Unnatural OHIO

A History of Buckeye Cryptids, Legends & Other Mysteries

M. Kristina Smith and Kevin Moore
Illustrations by Kari Schultz

THE
History
PRESS

Published by The History Press
Charleston, SC
www.historypress.com

Cover and internal illustrations by Kari Schultz.

First published 2023
Updated printing 2024

Manufactured in the United States

ISBN 9781467151443

Library of Congress Control Number: 2023937211

For Kevin's wife, Bethany, who has supported his writing aspirations since day one.

For Kristina's parents, Al and Faith Smith, who have always encouraged her creativity, writing and interest in the unexplained.

And for anyone who has ever believed they saw something truly extraordinary and were brave enough to talk about it.

CONTENTS

ACKNOWLEDGEMENTS

Many people made this book possible, and we, the authors, are so grateful to them for their help, support and encouragement.

This book resulted from a special exhibit at the museum where we work, the Hayes Presidential Library and Museums, in Fremont, Ohio. The exhibit, called *Ohio: An Unnatural History*, shared, in an abbreviated way, some of the stories mentioned here. It was one of the museum's most popular special exhibits. We want to thank Christie Weininger, the Hayes Presidential Library's executive director, and all of our coworkers for their support of the exhibit and this book project.

We'd also like to thank our editor at The History Press, John Rodrigue, for his continued help, feedback and support on the project. John helped us through all of our questions, from writing and editing to artwork, and worked with us through every step of this process.

Thank you to everyone who was interviewed for this book and told their stories and shared their expertise and insight, and thank you to those who shared and suggested reliable sources. We also want to recognize the many people who came forward when they saw something extraordinary and the reporters, authors and others who recorded these stories so there is still an excellent record of them today.

Thank you to everyone who assisted us with photographs and artwork. Finding photographs for a book about creatures that are not confirmed to exist, UFOs and the paranormal is not an easy task. We appreciate everyone who helped us out with the photographs that help tell these stories.

Several archives and libraries helped in researching and obtaining artwork for this book. We want to thank the Hayes Presidential Library, the Bowling Green State University Center for Archival Collections, the BGSU Ray and Pat Browne Library for Popular Culture Studies, the Center for UFO Studies, the National Investigations Committee on Aerial Phenomena, the Alpena County George N. Fletcher Public Library, the Ohio History Connection Archives and Library and the Missionary Church Archives and Historical Collections.

We would also like to thank Kent and Janet McClary, who worked on the paranormal radio show *Dead Air* on WBGSU for sixteen years. From recommending sources to helping connect us with people and having us on the show to talk about our project and these legends, they have been enthusiastic supporters of our work.

Thank you to Dustin McLochlin, the Hayes Presidential Library historian, who helped edit one of the chapters for this book.

We appreciate Bethany Moore of Breakthrough Images Photography for taking the time to photograph and edit our author headshots.

We also want to thank our families, who have always been encouraging and deeply supportive of this project and our interest in the topics presented here. We are so grateful to them for continuing to champion our work. Kristina would like to thank John Popson III; Al and Faith Smith; Jennifer Smith-Margraf, Joe Margraf and Samantha Margraf; Priscilla and John Popson Jr.; and her extended family and friends. Kevin would like to thank his wife, Bethany, for her encouragement (and patience), his children for thinking weird things like Bigfoot and Mothman are the "coolest" and the rest of his family and friends for their support that he would one day write a book.

And to all of you who find these topics interesting, regardless of whether you believe in the supernatural, thank you. You are the reason we wrote this book, and we hope you enjoy learning more about these beloved stories and legends.

INTRODUCTION

Abbout two in every three people reading this will likely believe in at least one of the supernatural Ohio legends we cover in this book. It would be a stretch to assume that they will believe the ghost of a headless motorcyclist haunts a country bridge in northwestern Ohio *and* that a serpentine monster stalks ships beneath the waters of Lake Erie *and* that a UFO piloted by aliens led Ohio police officers on a sixty-mile chase across the Pennsylvania border. But the odds are pretty good that two-thirds of the people thumbing through these pages will believe in at least *one* of those paranormal things.

Dr. Christopher Bader is a professor of sociology at Chapman University in Orange, California. Through work at both Chapman and Baylor Universities, Bader and a team of sociologists have conducted a series of nationwide polls through Gallup called the Baylor Religious Survey and the Chapman University Survey of American Fears to assess Americans' spiritual beliefs and what things cause Americans the most anxiety.

Every two or three years, Bader's research team included sections asking Americans about their beliefs related to ghosts, UFOs and aliens, Bigfoot and a host of other paranormal topics. They found that about 67 percent, a strong majority, of people in the United States believe in at least *something* paranormal. For example, someone may accept the idea of aliens visiting Earth but think ghosts are nonsense or vice versa.

Bader and his colleagues expounded on their team's research in the fascinating 2017 book *Paranormal America: Ghost Encounters, UFO Sightings, Bigfoot*

Hunts, and Other Curiosities in Religion and Culture, in which they dissected the survey data in all kinds of interesting ways. Overall, belief in the paranormal, or "paranormalism," is on the rise in America. Men and women gravitate toward different paranormal beliefs, with men being more accepting of "physical" things, like Bigfoot or aliens, and women being more accepting of "ethereal" ideas like ghosts or astrology. Paranormalism tends to decrease with age. Atheists and the most devout are less open to paranormal belief than those who are somewhat religious.

What this tells us is that paranormalism is complex. People believe what they do for a range of reasons that are as diverse as they are. Likewise, we understand that readers will approach this book from different places along the spectrum of paranormal belief.

When it comes to the paranormal, believers and nonbelievers alike tend to filter information through their worldview. This is not too dissimilar to how liberals and conservatives understand the news through their respective ideologies. For the authors, it doesn't particularly matter if the subjects of this book are real or not. We have tried our best to tell these stories and explain their histories as neutrally and objectively as possible. Are there ghosts of orphans haunting the woods around Gore Orphanage Road in northeastern Ohio? Is there a Frogman lurking in the Little Miami River? We're not going to attempt to prove or disprove these stories either way.

What matters to us is that real people have believed in things like the Ohio Grassman and Mothman, and the very presence of those beliefs means that there is a compelling history behind each of these legends that is well worth diving into. Communities all around the state of Ohio have incorporated supernatural folklore into their cultures, and in that way, these stories end up touching everyone, regardless of whether they believe in them.

It is fair to say our interests, as authors, have been greatly influenced by this cultural embrace of the supernatural. Each of us developed an interest in paranormal subjects early on, with Kevin growing up watching *The X-Files* and, later, *Supernatural* and Kristina checking out books on Bigfoot and the Loch Ness Monster from the city public library and watching *Unsolved Mysteries*. Along the way, we've both seen plenty of "proof" of the supernatural that isn't very convincing and listened to trusted friends whose strange experiences are difficult to ignore. Our relationship with the paranormal seems pretty similar to most Americans', at least according to Bader in *Paranormal America*: "They are simultaneously fascinated and repulsed, intrigued and dismissive."

The impetus for this book goes back to 2018, when we were involved in planning the upcoming exhibit schedule for the Rutherford B. Hayes Presidential Library and Museums in Fremont, Ohio, where Kevin works as a curator of artifacts and Kristina works as a marketing and communications manager. We noticed tremendous public interest in the museum's supernatural-themed programming around Halloween that retold local ghost stories and explored the history behind the occult and spiritualist movements during President Rutherford B. Hayes's lifetime. How, we wondered, could a presidential museum engage with such a fringe yet popular subject like the paranormal while offering something grounded in history?

The result was an exhibit that explored some of Ohio's most popular folktales and urban legends, which opened in the spring of 2020. While President Hayes was not a paranormalist in the slightest, he was a proud Ohioan, a history buff and a voracious reader who loved good stories. Our goal was to craft an exhibit (and now a book) that he would have found intriguing.

Unnatural Ohio greatly expands on the research we did for that exhibit. The book is broken into three sections, each dealing with different branches of the paranormal. The first deals with cryptozoological (cryptid) creatures, animals or "monsters" whose existence have not been proven that are said to prowl the state. The next looks at a sampling of Ohio's many ghost legends. Some are famous statewide, while others are local treasures. Finally, the last section covers the Buckeye State's most influential UFO cases.

Most of the folktales and legends covered in this book have been told and retold for years. In *Unnatural Ohio*, we try to avoid offering yet another retelling and instead determine where these legends might have originated and why they're relevant today. In some cases, we have learned that the way these stories get told has changed over time, and we try to track the course of that evolution. In many instances, we found communities that have embraced their legends as part of their identity and heritage.

We hope that anyone reading *Unnatural Ohio*, including that one-in-three person who discounts all things paranormal as bunk, will find our work enjoyable and learn something new about the Buckeye State.

PART I

BUCKEYE CRYPTIDS

1

BIGFOOT

Rumors that a hairy, naked "wild man" with crazed, bulging eyes was stalking the woods near Gallipolis had been circulating for several days in early 1869.

A group of women said the beast chased them down the road and nearly caught them. Thankfully for them, a wagon suddenly came down the road and startled the creature. Yelling loudly, it ran off into the woods outside the Southwest Ohio town just across the Ohio River from West Virginia.

Three young men who had been out hunting also reported seeing the creature.

Most locals didn't pay much attention to these stories until the wild man attacked a father and his teenage girl while their carriage passed through the same woods.

The father told the *Gallipolis Bulletin* it was near dark when he decided to get out of the carriage to give the horse pulling it a rest. His seventeen-year-old daughter, described by the newspaper as a "pretty and interesting girl," walked with the horse a few hundred yards ahead of the carriage.

"Suddenly, at a place where a turn in the road concealed the vehicle from his view, he was surprised by hearing two or three yells and whoops in his rear, and shortly afterwards the terrified screams and cries for help in his daughter's familiar voice," the newspaper reported.

He rushed ahead to see her struggling with the creature. When it saw the father, it left the girl and attacked him instead. The beast grabbed the father with a vice-like grip, threw him on the ground and began biting and scratching at him.

"The struggle was long and fearful, rolling and wallowing in the deep mud, half suffocated, sometimes beneath his adversary, whose burning and maniac eyes glared into his own with murderous and savage intensity," according to the article, which was reprinted on January 23, 1869, in the *Burlington* (VT) *Free Press.*

The daughter then hurled a rock at the beast, pelting it in the head.

"The creature was not stunned, but feeling unequal to further exertion, slowly got up and retired into a neighboring copse that skirted the road," the newspaper reported. "As soon as the gentleman had sufficiently recovered he, with the help of his daughter, continued his journey to the city, where he arrived after dark, exhausted, cut, and bleeding from his severe wounds."

The father and daughter's harrowing escape from the wild man is believed to be the first newspaper account of one of Ohio's most famous creature legends. At that time, the creatures were called wild men or reported as gorillas and apes that had escaped from circuses or zoos. Today, they are known as Bigfoot, Sasquatch and, sometimes in Ohio, Grassman.

The ape-like creature, traditionally described as being between six and eight feet tall and covered in hair, resembling a primate, has been spotted for decades across the United States, including throughout the Buckeye State.

Ohio ranks fourth in the United States for the highest number of Bigfoot sightings. Only Washington, California and Florida have more reports of Bigfoot sightings, the *Cincinnati Enquirer* reported on August 5, 2022.

"There has been such a long tradition of sasquatch in Ohio," said Micah Hanks, who runs the podcast *Sasquatch Tracks* and is the author and founder of the Debrief, a website that focuses on scientific news and mysteries. "There's been a long-held focus on that topic, which has everything from a potential scientific interest to a potential marketability."

SIGHTINGS OF "WILD MEN" AND APES

At the time of the carriage incident near Gallipolis, the name "Bigfoot" didn't exist yet. Stories of wild men were common in newspapers throughout the country, and Ohio was no exception.

In nearly every part of the state, the stories of strange, naked men covered in matted hair and ape-like creatures were reported through the 1930s, according to Chad Arment's *The Historical Bigfoot*, a compilation of newspaper reports of sightings of Bigfoot-like creatures before the name "Bigfoot" became popularized.

Bigfoot. *Illustration by Kari Schultz.*

In most of the Ohio sightings, these wild men were not as aggressive as the one in the 1869 Gallipolis carriage incident. Most often, the creature appeared to be looking for food in berry patches and gardens or spotted in the woods.

The *Hartford* (CT) *Courant* reported on December 15, 1883, that two hunters had a run-in with an animal that was covered in hair and looked like a gorilla in Calcutta, a small burg in Columbiana County along the Ohio–Pennsylvania border. The forest where they encountered the animal was very dense with hills and caves and was a popular hiding spot for criminals who were avoiding the law.

The hunters heard a strange cry and saw the creature run out of a rocky area. It stared at them for a few minutes, cried again and ran into the woods. One of the men fired his gun and hit the creature in the arm.

"It turned with a horrible scream of rage and pursued the hunters, who threw away their guns and ran at the top of their speed," the *Courant* reported. "The creature gained on them until they reached a clearing and a fence, over which they jumped. The animal then ran back into the woods."

For about a week in 1930, residents of Norwalk, a city just south of Sandusky, locked their doors and stayed inside while one hundred armed men searched for an ape on the loose in the area.

On June 6, 1930, there was a flurry of sightings around the town. Some saw the beast near the hospital, and others saw it in a farmer's garden and around a nearby swimming pool. A group from Detroit spotted it along the highway near their car after they ran out of gas, according to newspaper articles published in the *Elyria Chronicle Telegram* on June 6 and in the *Independent* in Helena, Montana, on June 7, 1930.

"John Goodsite of Milan, Ohio, patient at the Memorial Hospital, Norwalk, told of hearing a hoarse scream in the night," the Associated Press reported in an article published on June 7, 1930, in the *Sunday Star* of Washington, D.C. "He looked out of the window and saw an ungainly, fur-covered animal ambling into the woods at the rear of the hospital."

Hospital janitor John Remele told the Associated Press that "some beast of unusual strength" had twisted the posts and wires of the hospital's chicken coop and reached inside to kill many of the chickens.

For days, an armed posse searched the Norwalk area for the creature, which the *Chronicle-Telegram* reported was likely an ape escaped from a circus, but found no trace of the animal. Newspaper reports at that time indicated the creature might have moved west, with sightings reported near Fremont and Alger, a small village near Lima.

MODERN BIGFOOT SIGHTINGS

In the 1920s, J.W. Burns, a teacher at a First Nations reservation in British Columbia, Canada, popularized the name "Sasquatch" in reference to a wild man that had been reported in the area. Sasquatch is an anglicized version of a word from a British Columbian First Nations language.

Then in 1958, the name "Bigfoot" entered the popular lexicon, and newspaper accounts began using this name in articles about creature sightings.

Another name for Bigfoot that is sometimes used in Ohio is "Grassman." This name originated in Akron in the 1980s, according to Marc DeWerth, a Bigfoot investigator of Columbia Station, near Cleveland. Residents there saw a hairy, ape-like creature and dubbed it Grassman, the *Akron Beacon Journal* reported on January 29, 2001. DeWerth, however, prefers the names Bigfoot or Sasquatch, as Grassman relates to an isolated area and group of sightings.

Whatever they are called, sightings of these creatures have persisted throughout the past seventy years.

The Bigfoot Field Researchers Organization (BFRO) has been publishing reports of sightings online since 1995, and it has reports from 75 percent of the state's counties. In each case, BFRO sends out an investigator to interview witnesses and examine the sighting area.

"Every so often, you get legitimacy," said DeWerth, a BFRO Ohio field curator. "For every ten calls, you were lucky to get one that was good."

Portage, Columbiana and Guernsey Counties, all rural areas of eastern Ohio, have the highest number of reported sightings recorded with the BFRO. One of the most popular Bigfoot areas in the state is Salt Fork State Park, located in the Appalachian hills of Guernsey County.

DeWerth said he had his own run-in with Bigfoot in April 1997 in southern Coshocton County in east-central Ohio, off State Route 410. It was during the day, and he had been hiking in the woods.

Janet McClary, the cohost of the paranormal radio show *Dead Air* in Northwest Ohio, holds a cast of a footprint believed to have been left by a bigfoot at Salt Fork State Park. *Kristina Smith.*

"It basically followed me out of the woods," he said. "I thought it was a cougar stalking me, because there were reports of a big cat in the area at that time."

DeWerth turned and saw something squatted down on the slope. At first, he thought it was a black bear.

"It stands up and turns its shoulder and turns its torso, and I could see its ear," said DeWerth, who still regrets that he didn't have a video camera with him. "It was the most beautiful thing I've ever seen. It looked so healthy. It was so massive and muscular."

COULD BIGFOOT REALLY EXIST?

In the world of Bigfoot and Sasquatch, hoaxes, like those including fake footprints and gorilla suits, have been common.

Even some of the historical newspaper accounts are likely fabrications that were used for slow news days, which was not uncommon in the late 1800s, Hanks said. Arment points out in his book that some of the wild man sightings were probably just sightings of humans who were hermits living in the woods.

In 2008, two men in Georgia went as far as to claim they had found a Bigfoot corpse, only to have DNA testing show it was a rubber gorilla costume, according to an article news service Reuters published on August 20, 2008.

For those who study Bigfoot phenomena, viewing everything with a skeptical eye is essential to weeding out obvious hoodwinks and finding credible reports.

"There's a long tradition of hoaxing in the [United States]," Hanks said. "What's often left out of the discussion is that if we go all the way back to the 1850s to the 1870s, there are historical accounts that very actually match the modern description of Sasquatch. Creatures just don't spring into existence in modern time. There's a historical basis and quite a rich one."

Hanks said that looking past the hoaxes, there are too many credible reports—especially from witnesses who have more to lose than they have to gain by sharing their stories—to rule out the existence of Sasquatch.

Many who study Bigfoot classify themselves in different ways.

There are knowers, like DeWerth, who said he knows Bigfoot is real because he has seen one. He believes there is a small population of Sasquatches in Ohio, at least enough to be reproducing.

There are believers, like Hanks, who believe the creature exists because he has spoken with witnesses, such as U.S. Department of Forestry and U.S. Department of the Interior workers whose careers could be negatively

Hosak's Cave has been a hot spot for bigfoot sightings over the years at Salt Fork State Park. *Kristina Smith.*

Salt Fork State Park is Ohio's largest state park and includes acres of remote woods. This photograph was taken on the Morgan's Knob trail. *Kristina Smith.*

impacted by speaking about their experiences—yet they have come forward anyway.

And there are those, like Salt Fork State Park Naturalist John Hickenbottom, who are skeptical but entertain the possibility Bigfoot is a real, scientific creature yet to be positively confirmed.

"I'm firmly on the fence about Bigfoot," said Hickenbottom, who works for the Ohio Department of Natural Resources.

Hickenbottom, who is from the Cambridge area and grew up hunting at Salt Fork, first became a naturalist at the park in 2016. He was very dismissive of any Bigfoot talk at the time. After he started talking with visitors who reported strange sounds and sightings and working more with Bigfoot researchers on hikes, his thoughts on the subject began to change.

"It became really hard for me to dismiss things," he said. "I became much more fascinated on it. I felt like this warranted more research."

Hickenbottom himself has had a couple experiences that made him question what might have been out in the woods. In 2018, he and his future wife were squirrel hunting in the park when they heard a long, mournful

Morgan's Knob is another spot where there have been several bigfoot sightings at Salt Fork State Park. *Kristina Smith.*

howl from a distance in the woods. It was a howl they had not heard before in nature, and it matched a recording of a howl caught with an audio recorder in Columbiana County reputed to be made by a Bigfoot.

It could have been a Bigfoot hunter playing the recording to attract a Bigfoot, which Hickenbottom said is always possible at Salt Fork.

His second experience occurred in March 2021, when he was making a video for the park, and he heard a wood knock. Bigfoot researchers across the country have speculated that Sasquatches knock on trees to communicate with each other or give warning signs to intruders.

"In the middle of the video, while I'm talking, it sounds like a home run," Hickenbottom said. "It was in March. It was not an acorn dropping out of a tree. It sounds like it's just inside the woods. It made me uneasy."

His own experiences aside, Hickenbottom hears almost weekly from park visitors who have some sort of unusual experience. He encounters everyone from Bigfoot hunters to families enjoying a long weekend away in nature.

"I'm more interested in the thirty-something dad or mom who has no skin in the Bigfoot game," he said. "I'm more interested in the people who were out for a day hike and saw something that shook them up."

Yet Hickenbottom, Hanks and DeWerth acknowledge that without a body, skeleton or some sort of biological evidence, Bigfoot sounds and sightings remain just that: unconfirmed phenomena. Many footprint casts have been taken that are purported to be from the creature, but none have been confirmed as belonging to anything that science hasn't already identified.

For believers, the lack of a recovered Sasquatch body or skeleton doesn't mean the animal is mythical. Salt Fork, Ohio's largest state park with 17,229 acres, and other parts of eastern Ohio are very remote, with hills, caves and bluffs that could conceal any animal and quickly decompose its remains after death.

"I'm not as interested in finding physical evidence of Bigfoot as I am the phenomena itself," Hickenbottom said. "I think a lot of times people just want to tell their stories."

CAPITALIZING ON INTEREST IN SQUATCHIN'

Regardless of whether Bigfoot actually exists, the stories and sightings of Bigfoot have created a huge amount of public interest. For many areas reputed to be home to Sasquatch, there is an opportunity to capitalize on that enthusiasm, Hanks said.

Salt Fork is the site of the annual Ohio Bigfoot Conference, which Don Keating started in the 1980s in Newcomerstown and DeWerth took over in 2011. The conference moved to Salt Fork in the early 2000s.

The conference has four hundred spots, and they usually sell out within a few minutes of registration opening, DeWerth said. During the conference

Left: A giant wood carving of bigfoot welcomes you to the lounge at the Salt Fork State Park Lodge. *Kristina Smith*.

Below: These woods on Salt Fork Lake near the Kennedy Stone House Museum are known for bigfoot sightings. *Kristina Smith*.

weekend, three thousand to five thousand people come to Salt Fork to visit the vendor tables and hike the trails. The conference also offers a closing event that is open to the public for those who couldn't get tickets to interact with some of the speakers.

In addition to the attention the conference brought the park, interest in Salt Fork's squatchiness also increased in the early 2010s after the TV shows *Finding Bigfoot* and *MonsterQuest* filmed episodes there, Hickenbottom said.

The park itself has embraced Bigfoot mania. Maps with recent sightings, as well as Sasquatch hot spot areas in the park, are available at the lodge's front desk. The gift shop is filled with T-shirts, sweatshirts, books and other Salt Fork Bigfoot swag.

Hickenbottom offers Bigfoot hikes, which attract hundreds of people. Although Sasquatch is the main draw, Hickenbottom fits a large amount of information about confirmed Ohio creatures, from birds and butterflies to snakes and plants into each event.

"That's an interesting thing to me, seeing the way that the park and park officials use that, with really John kind of leading the charge with this," Hanks said. "No matter what you think about Sasquatch, there is an opportunity to get people outside and involved with nature, get them out and exercising and having an appreciation for nature."

Salt Fork isn't the only spot in the state that draws Bigfoot enthusiasts. In 2022, the first Hocking Hills Bigfoot Festival took place in Logan in Central Ohio. Hocking Hills is another popular wooded destination with remote areas.

For many, their interest in Bigfoot continues to grow because Bigfoot represents an unknown in a time where technology increasingly makes the world a smaller place.

"It's a very American thing in that you have this creature that you can't even get a good photo of," Hickenbottom said. "It's wild. It doesn't care about elections. It doesn't care about football games."

If Bigfoot were ever confirmed as a biological creature, this would be a huge scientific breakthrough. But it also would be somewhat sad, because the mystery would be over, Hickenbottom said.

"I think having that mystery out there fascinates people and comforts people," Hickenbottom said. "We still need mysteries."

2

THE LOVELAND FROG

Southwestern Ohio is home to a legend that even paranormal enthusiasts describe as a "strange case." This tale comes from the vicinity around Loveland, a community that straddles Hamilton, Warren and Clermont Counties. Today, this Cincinnati suburb of thirteen thousand people leans heavily into its nickname, the "Sweetheart of Ohio," with a small love-themed arts scene and a historic downtown district that caters to cyclists along the Little Miami Scenic Trail.

The paved bike trail, which has become a lifeline for the city, follows the Little Miami River for nearly eighty miles from Columbus to Cincinnati. The murky depths of Little Miami serve as the backdrop for a peculiar cryptid legend known as the Loveland Frog or Loveland Frogman.

One thing that makes the Loveland Frog so strange is that it does not follow the modus operandi of many other cryptid creatures. Most cryptid legends emerge from a large body of sightings in which people claim to have had similar encounters with the same creature. For example, year after year, people in southeastern Ohio report seeing a tall, hairy, ape-like being, and we have collectively decided to call this thing the Ohio Grassman. By contrast, the Loveland Frog seems to come from just three encounters spread decades apart.

Most coverage of the Loveland Frog in paranormal print literature or websites begins with a vague sighting near a bridge crossing the Little Miami River in 1955. The following passage from *Monsters of the Midwest: True*

Tales of Bigfoot, Werewolves & Other Legendary Creatures by Jessica Freeburg and Natalie Fowler is representative of most iterations:

> *Back in 1955…a businessman was driving late at night and saw three creatures on the side of Hopewell Road. They were three to four feet tall, and they stood up straight, on their hind legs. Their hands and feet were webbed, and they had heads and faces like frogs.…One of them held a wand, and it shot a spray of sparks.*

There seems to have been nothing more from the Loveland Frog for nearly two decades. In fact, there are no records that anyone in the 1960s was even circulating stories about a Frogman.

That all changed in 1972, when a series of encounters by local law enforcement cemented the legend into local folklore. On an evening in early March, a rookie patrolman for the Loveland Police Department named Ray Shockey saw a "three-foot-tall frog" near the Little Miami River. The first newspaper to cover the unusual story was the *Cincinnati Post and Times Star* on March 27, which described what Shockey saw as "an animal two to three feet tall with dark green or blackish scaly skin." According to the *Dayton Journal Herald*, reporting a few weeks later in April, Shockey shared his experience with only his commanding officers for fear of "raising alarm" (and perhaps incurring ridicule) in the community. Shockey refused to comment on the matter when contacted by the *Journal Herald*.

However, Shockey's partner Mark Matthews (sometimes appearing as Mark Mathews) felt comfortable speaking with the press about an encounter he had with the creature shortly before sunrise on St. Patrick's Day. According to the *Post and Times Star*, the twenty-one-year-old Matthews spotted the "two- to four-feet-high" creature about a quarter of a mile from where Shockey had seen it. Matthews said it was "irritated" and "stuck its tongue out at me.…It was forked like a serpent's." At that point, he said, he pulled his pistol and shot at the creature. He missed, and the thing fled.

Recalling the incident a few weeks later, Matthews told a slightly different story to the *Dayton Journal Herald*. Matthews told the newspaper that while he was driving along the river on Kemper Road, he "saw this thing about three feet long and with a face like a frog hop at me." He said the creature showed no signs of aggression against him, but still he decided to shoot it with his .357 Magnum. "It was running and I wanted to see what it was, so I fired at it, hit it four times," he said. Despite these wounds, the creature hopped away, down the embankment and into the river. When

A cartoonist's illustration of Mark Matthews's encounter. *From the* Dayton Journal Herald, *April 12, 1972.*

asked about "monsters," Matthews told the newspaper that he believed what he saw was a large iguana.

Despite not having any remains of the strange creature, the Loveland Police Department appears to have done their due diligence in trying to identify it. Both the *Post and Times Star* and the *Journal Herald* describe a composite sketch submitted by the police to the Cincinnati Zoo. The *Journal Herald* asked zoologist Parry Wakeman for his expert opinion, and he quickly dismissed the sketch as matching no known "possible" animal. While he acknowledged the existence of extremely large frogs that inhabit tropical regions, such as the West African giant frog, one could not survive the climate of Ohio in March. He speculated that perhaps what Matthews saw was a river otter or woodchuck.

An image purported to be that original sketch is in circulation on numerous websites, but we, the authors of this book, were unable to authenticate the legitimacy of the image. We contacted the Loveland Police Department to see what records they had on the case, but Chief of Police Dennis Rahe said that the department had no reports on file related to the Loveland Frog.

Within six short years of the officers' experience, the name "Loveland Frog" entered the lexicon of Ohio folklore, and the story began attracting its share of believers and skeptics. In June 1978, the *Dayton Daily News* ran a special feature in the leisure section of its Sunday edition titled "Monsters in Your Own Backyard" that profiled a series of cryptid creatures said to roam Southwest Ohio, including the Loveland Frog. The article's author, who clearly took these folktales with a large grain of salt, recounted Shockey and Matthews's testimony from a few years earlier but described the creature in much more humanoid terms: "[It resembled] the gillman from Hollywood's *Creature from the Black Lagoon*."

The Loveland Frog again went into hiding following the Shockey-Matthews sighting until a viral smartphone game breathed new life into the legend. When *Pokémon Go* was released in July 2016, the nation's teens and young adults spent the remainder of the summer wandering in a daze, their eyes glued to the augmented reality game on their smartphones, bumping into objects and occasionally getting arrested for trespassing. It was during this cultural phenomenon that Lovelander Sam Jacobs and his girlfriend found themselves hunting for Pokémon along the banks of Lake Isabella, a seventy-six-acre man-made lake situated within a park next to the Little Miami River. In an email sent to Cincinnati's ABC affiliate television station, WCPO, Jacobs described a bipedal humanoid creature that stood about four feet tall on its hind legs. "We saw a huge frog near the water," he said. "Not in the game—this was an actual giant frog."

Some of the paranormal literature attempts to anchor the Loveland Frog in the deep past by attaching it to Native mythology. The earliest source to suggest such a connection appears to be a 2012 book titled *It Came from Ohio: True Tales of the Weird*, by James Renner, a journalist from Cleveland. "Turns out the legend is older than anyone suspected. Much older," he writes. "Even Shockey didn't know about the first recorded sighting of the Loveland Frog, which occurred before the town of Loveland was even constructed." Renner goes on to describe interactions in the late seventeenth century between French missionaries and the Miami culture. Supposedly, the tribesmen warned the Frenchmen of a dangerous creature they called the Shawnahooc, a name that translates, according to Renner, to "river demon," with wrinkly skin and no nose.

Casual internet research will uncover numerous paranormal articles that paraphrase Renner's description of the Shawnahooc and recall the story of the French missionaries. However, these references appear only in relation to material on the Loveland Frog. Nothing matching the name or description of the Shawnahooc appears in external sources on Miami folklore or in the traditions of the related Shawnee or Algonquin cultures. As Ryan Haupt writes for the urban legend debunking podcast *Skeptoid*, "This represents little more than a likely false appeal to antiquity, or the wisdom of the ancients, as well as possibly attaching a bit of Sasquatch-esque significance to the Frogmen."

The Miami people did believe in a rich collection of several water-based entities, such as the Real Lynx, a fearsome cross between a lynx and a dragon that lived at the bottom of lakes, and the Maneto, a giant horned water serpent believed to inhabit North America's rivers. However, there is nothing to indicate the Loveland Frog has its origins with the Native people who once lived in southwestern Ohio and southern Indiana.

Most stories of the Loveland Frog attribute the first sighting in modern times to a businessman who was traveling through the region in 1955. Cryptozoologist Michael Newton identifies the mysterious businessman as Robert Hunnicutt in his 2013 book *Strange Ohio Monsters*. Newton's bibliography attributes his description of the encounter only to the ambiguously named "Humanoid Sighting Reports," but the name Robert Hunnicutt provides a significant clue that moves this piece of the Loveland Frog puzzle from the realm of cryptozoology to a different subgenre of the paranormal: ufology.

The 1950s and 1960s has been dubbed by some ufologists as the "Golden Age of Flying Saucers," because during this time, Americans frequently reported seeing lights and strange metallic craft in the sky. At the same time, several people across the country reported sightings of "little men" associated with these craft. Newspaper editors at the time associated these miniature beings with the cartoonish depictions of extraterrestrials in science-fiction pulp magazines of the 1930s and 1940s and began to refer to them disparagingly as "little green men." Probably the best known of these little green men stories is the Kelly-Hopkinsville encounter, in which a Kentucky family claimed to have a shootout with diminutive beings on their farm in 1955.

Little green men became a source of fascination for the American public, and newspapers from the time preserve op-eds in which believers and skeptics traded barbs over the issue. The United States Air Force appears to have taken some interest and sent members of its Project Blue Book UFO program to investigate the Kelly-Hopkinsville encounter. Enthusiasts and concerned citizens began forming civilian research groups to catalog and document these flying saucer and little green men sightings.

One such group was Civilian Research, Interplanetary Flying Objects (CRIFO), founded in 1954 by an advertising manager from Columbus named Leonard H. Stringfield. CRIFO published a newsletter from 1954 to 1957 called *ORBIT* that reported on developments in astronomy and aeronautics, shared the group's investigations into aerial phenomena and monitored the U.S. military's handling of the subject. Stringfield produced *ORBIT* from his home to disseminate information that he claimed came to him directly from the Air Force, which, he said, had designated his home as its official "UFO reporting post."

Stringfield first published what eventually became the first Loveland Frog encounter in the September 2, 1955 issue of *ORBIT* under the headline "The Controversial Little Green Men and the Tingling Facts." The article presents the Loveland sighting as one of several run-ins with little men being reported by witnesses who were finally willing to come forward after the Kelly-Hopkinsville encounter made national headlines. Stringfield declined to reveal the Loveland witness's identity, referring to him as the now-familiar "prominent businessman," but he briefly summarized the man's sighting of "four 'strange little men about three feet tall' under a certain bridge."

Stringfield provided considerably more detail two years later when he published *Inside Saucer Post…3–0 BLUE: CRIFO Views the Status Quo: A Summary Report*, a semiautobiographical account of CRIFO's research. In *Saucer Post*, Stringfield writes about an investigation that was conducted in August 1956 by himself and fellow CRIFO member Ted Bloecher, in which they followed up on several reported little men sightings in the Cincinnati area.

The pair first visited Loveland Police Chief John Fritz to discuss the bridge incident. Chief Fritz was reluctant to discuss the issue, as it was supposedly being investigated by the FBI, but he did provide the witness's name, which Stringfield printed in *Saucer Post* as "C.F." Unfortunately, C.F. was unwilling to speak to Stringfield and Bloecher when they showed up at his door later that day.

While the "bridge affair" had apparently reached a dead end, Chief Fritz gave the investigators some new information that would later find its way into the Loveland Frog mythos. He relayed a separate encounter reported by an "R.H." while he was driving just outside of Loveland:

> *About 4 a.m. on a March night in* [1955], *while driving through Branch Hill on his way to Loveland, R.H. saw in the beams of his headlights, what appeared to be three men kneeling at the right side of the road.… Curious, he stopped his car and got out for a better look. To his surprise,*

he discovered that the figures were non-human and about three feet tall. They were not green, R.H. stressed, but rather a "greyish color" including the garments. These tight-fitting [clothes] stretched over a "lop-sided chest" which bulged at the shoulder to the arm pit.…"Their heads were ugly," said R.H., reminding him of a "frog's face" mostly because of the mouth which spanned, in a thin line, across a smooth grey face. While R.H. thought the eyes, "without brows" seemed normal and the "nose was indistinct," the pate of the head "had a painiet-on-like-hair effect, like a plastic doll."

According to R.H., the middle biped, and the one closest to him, was first seen, with his arms upraised. "They were raised a foot or so above the head," he said, "and holding a dark chain or stick, which emitted blue white sparks jumping from one hand to the other."…R.H. said he wanted to get closer, but by the time he had reached the front fender of his car the "little men" made a slight "un-natural" move toward him, "as if motioning me not to come any closer."

Ted Bloecher later cowrote a book with Isabel Davis on the national "little man flap" titled *Close Encounters at Kelly and Others of 1955*, produced by the Center for UFO Studies in 1976. The book dedicated three exhaustive chapters to little man encounters around Cincinnati, including "The Loveland Case." Bloecher's account of the Loveland bridge sighting offers few new details about the bridge encounter other than the fact that the witness, C.F., was not a businessman at all but rather a nineteen-year-old member of the Loveland Ground Observer Corps, a civil defense organization that built fallout shelters and held drills for Hamilton County to prepare for the possibility of nuclear war with the Soviet Union.

However, *Close Encounters at Kelly* does more fully develop the little men sighting at Branch Hill. Bloecher reveals that R.H. was Robert Hunnicutt, a short-order cook working in Loveland. He writes that he and Stringfield interviewed Hunnicutt in 1956 and that Stringfield drew an original sketch of the little men based on Hunnicutt's description. This un-frog-like depiction serves as the earliest visual interpretation of what Hunnicutt claimed he saw.

What is noticeably absent in Davis and Bloecher's 1976 reflections is any mention of Ray Shockey and Mark Matthews's experience just a few years earlier in 1972. Similarly, none of the early newspapers that reported on the Shockey-Matthews sightings made any mention of the "little man flap" seen around Cincinnati twenty years beforehand in the mid-1950s. If any of these writers were aware of both events, they did not connect them.

A sketch of the "frog-like" beings reported by Robert Hunnicutt in 1955, as drawn in an interview by Leonard Stringfield in 1956. *Center for UFO Studies*.

It is clear that the first alleged appearance of the Loveland Frog doesn't deal with an amphibious cryptid at all. These are a set of stories about supposed extraterrestrial visitations that were later appropriated, fused together and distorted as the Loveland Frog legend evolved.

The Hunnicutt sighting is not the only part of Loveland Frog folklore to undergo revision over the years. When Sam Jacobs saw the Loveland Frog in 2016, the news piqued the interest of none other than Patrolman Mark Matthews, who had since retired to Florida. He contacted WCPO the day after it published its initial article on Jacobs's encounter to weigh in on the sighting. Matthews said that his experience occurred about three weeks after Shockey's, and he emphasized that what he saw in 1972 was not bipedal and did not stand upright.

"I know no one would believe me, so I shot it," he told WCPO. "The thing was half dead anyway when I shot it." Matthews recalled hitting a large three-feet-long iguana that was missing its tail and putting its body in the trunk of his police car to show Shockey. He speculated that the lizard was using the discharge pipes of a nearby factory to keep warm during the winter months. "It's a big hoax. There's a logical explanation for everything," he said.

Matthews has been trying to clarify what he saw by the river in Loveland for years. For a 1999 article titled "True Tale of Loveland's 'Monster'" in the *Cincinnati Post*, an "exasperated" Matthews complained that reporters had never been interested in what he had to say. Matthews told WCPO in 2016 that he tried to officially put the story to rest by providing quotes for a recent book on urban legends, but the book's author selectively omitted the portions of his interview that did not fit the cryptid creature narrative.

Some paranormal sources, such as Weird U.S. and Cryptid Wiki, claim Matthews changed his story years after the fact and speculate that perhaps he just wanted to avoid the stigma that is sometimes felt by many who experience the paranormal. While Matthews is on record as early as April 1972 suggesting that what he saw was actually an iguana, other parts of his testimony have never been wholly consistent.

In the immediate reporting following the alleged incident, Matthews is quoted in one newspaper saying he missed the creature after shooting at it when it lunged at him and then is quoted in another newspaper saying he repeatedly shot and hit the creature for no other reason than his own curiosity. Even Matthews's later efforts to set the record straight contain noticeable discrepancies. In 2001, he told *X-Project Paranormal Magazine* that after he shot the "lizard," it crawled away, where "it either died of the wound

Frogman. *Illustration by Kari Schultz.*

or eventually died from the cold weather." This is considerably different from what he told WCPO fifteen years later, when he claimed he put the creature's carcass in the trunk of his car to show his partner.

For his part, Ray Shockey has been considerably less vocal on the issue. James Renner caught up with Shockey while writing *It Came from Ohio*. He told Renner that he had sworn off talking about the incident for a long time, because "it gave [him] so much grief." Shockey's mother once told a reporter for the *Cincinnati Post* that "Ray took so much ridicule over that thing that he stopped giving interviews a long time ago."

But Renner was able to get Shockey to offer at least one comment about the incident, which Renner relays in somewhat dramatic fashion: "I will tell you this much. It wasn't a frog. Wasn't an iguana, either.…It was…bigger."

Today, as expected, believers in the paranormal trust in Shockey's continued insistence that he saw something extraordinary, whereas skeptics have latched onto Matthews's denial as the final word in an open-and-shut case.

The 2016 Jacobs encounter, on the other hand, has raised eyebrows across the board. Jacobs sent WCPO a photograph and short video from his phone as proof of what he saw. As is often the case with the evidence presented in paranormal cases, Jacobs's images are low-resolution and inconclusive at best. Online skeptics quickly pointed out that the creature's eyes seem to be emitting their own light rather than reflecting the light from the phone's flash. One blogger even found a decorative Halloween statue from the discount store Big Lots shaped like a frog and sporting large, round glasses that house LED lights. The consensus from most seems to be that this evidence of the Loveland Frog is probably a hoax.

Whether the Frogman is an alien, cryptid or a figment of sheer imagination, Loveland has embraced it with open arms. Local coffee shop Mile 42 Coffee offers a Frogman latte and has incorporated the Loveland Frog into its merchandising. Another local eatery, Hometown Cafe Loveland, offers a healthy (and very green) kale, spinach, kiwi, banana and avocado smoothie called the Frogman. Starting in 2014, each September, local athletes participate in the Loveland Frogman Race, a triathlon that combines five miles of canoeing or kayaking on the Little Miami River with an eight-mile bicycle course and a 5K run. The Loveland Frog also served as the namesake for an acoustic rock and indie folk music festival held at the Loveland Castle, a local landmark, in 2017.

Hugo West Theatricals, a comedy playwright company based in Cincinnati, even produced a bluegrass musical called *Hot Damn! It's the Loveland Frog!* The theatrical troupe has received numerous awards for its farcical productions, such as *Don't Cross the Streams*, a spoof of *Ghostbusters*, and *Harambe*, a tribute the Cincinnati Zoo's gorilla that went viral after being shot by authorities in 2016. In *Hot Damn! It's the Loveland Frog!*, a bluegrass band accompaniment follows the raucous adventures of "maniacal moonshiners, crooked cops and the last Twightwee Indian as they rescue Pee Paw from the wondrous and elusive Loveland Frog." The production received glowing accolades from critics when it played at the Cincinnati Fringe Festival in 2014.

In 1985, Edgar Slotkin, a professor of folklore at the University of Cincinnati, told the *Gadsden Times* that urban legends like that of the Loveland Frog tend to be cyclical. At the time, in the mid-1980s, no one had seen the creature since Shockey and Matthews's reported sighting thirteen years earlier. Slotkin said, "I expect it to show up fairly soon." Since the Frogman just recently captured the public imagination in 2016, believers may have to wait a while before it's spotted in the river again. But until then, it will no doubt remain an evergreen feature around downtown Loveland.

3

THE DOGMAN OF DEFIANCE

In the early morning on July 25, 1972, Ted Davis was working on railcars at the Norfolk and Western yard in Defiance.

The moon was nearly full, and the yard, located behind an industrial plant, was quiet.

"I was connecting an air hose between two cars and was looking down," Davis, a railroad worker from Toledo, told the *Toledo Blade* in an article published August 2, 1972. "I saw these huge, hairy feet. Then I looked up, and he was standing there with a big stick over his shoulder."

The "he" Davis described was a hairy creature with the head of a dog, standing upright at six to eight feet tall and wearing blue jeans, like a human.

"When I started to say something, he took off for the woods," Davis said.

This was one of the first sightings of what is today known as the Dogman of Defiance. The canine-man would terrorize Defiance for a few days in July and August 1972, sending residents of this Northwest Ohio city built around the confluence of the Maumee and Auglaize Rivers into werewolf hysteria.

Police were flooded with calls from scared residents who thought the creature was scratching on their houses or following them. Others had their guns ready in case they had a run-in with the beast.

As suddenly as the sightings started, the Dogman disappeared. Today, the Dogman of Defiance is one of Ohio's most famous legends.

The Sightings

After Davis saw the creature, he told coworker and fellow Toledoan Tom Jones. Skeptical, Jones thought Davis was pranking him.

Jones quickly changed his mind after he, too, saw the creature with Davis a few days later on July 30 in the railyard. Again clad in jeans, the beast was standing on some weeds near the main railroad track, the pair told the *Blade*.

Jones could account for all the rail crewmen at the time, so he knew none of them were playing a joke. He and Davis, who worked an overnight train run through the city at the time, also said the creature had fangs and ran from side to side, "like a caveman in the movies," according to the newspaper.

As the spooked rail workers ran from the creature, they heard screams coming from a car that had stopped on one of the nearby streets, presumably from someone else who had seen it.

"That thing's going to hurt somebody someday," Jones told the *Blade*.

The railyard where the sightings occurred is located at the intersection of Fifth Street and Harrison Avenue, a few blocks from the Maumee River. Thick brush lines the railroad tracks, which continue to a rail bridge over the

Dogman. *Illustration by Kari Schultz.*

Brush still lines part of the railroad tracks in the area where a railroad worker reported seeing the Dogman run off. *Kristina Smith.*

Maumee, offering cover for whatever frightened the rail workers. This area likely was "the woods" Davis referenced.

The neighborhood was and remains residential with some industrial spots and is located three blocks from the city's downtown area.

The *Blade* and the *Crescent-News*, the local Defiance paper, also reported that the creature hit one of the rail workers on the shoulder with a two-by-four, or board, although none of the accounts specifically identify which worker was assaulted. Davis and Jones are the only witnesses identified in both newspapers.

Police reports from the time are not digitized and are archived as paper copies in boxes in the department's storage. They are searchable only by the name of the person who filed them, and the police department has no reports under Davis's or Jones's names.

The *Crescent-News* and *Blade* accounts, however, preserve the story of the Dogman and give a window into the investigation and townspeople's reaction.

POLICE INVESTIGATE

When the first sighting of the creature was reported, the Defiance Police Department didn't know what to make of it and didn't initially release it to the media, Donald Breckler, the police chief at the time, told the *Blade*.

"But now we're taking it seriously," Breckler told the newspaper on August 2, 1972. "We're concerned for the safety of our people."

Witnesses reported the creature was very tall and wearing "some kind of animal head," according to a *Crescent-News* article, also published on August 2. By the time the article was published, there had been three sightings of the creature, and police were looking for the Dogman between 1:00 and 4:00 a.m. around the railyard at Fifth Street.

The third sighting came from an employee of the Chief grocery store on Deatrick Street, a few blocks south of the railyard. The employee was driving in the area around 4:00 a.m. and saw the creature run in front of his car and then disappear, according to the *Blade*.

The *Crescent-News* played up the similarities between these sightings and werewolf stories with the headline "Horror Movie Now Playing on Fifth St." but included in the article that "no one has reported neck bites."

Breckler thought the werewolf, described in *Blade* accounts as being seven to nine feet tall, was actually a local person wearing a mask, although he did add "there was a lot of natural hair, too." He speculated that the person lived in the neighborhood around the railyard or was riding around on trains that stopped at the yard.

The person's motive, however, was a mystery.

"If his motive is robbery, then he is not picking on the type of person that would have a lot of money," Breckler told the *Blade* in a follow-up article on August 4. "If [publicity is] what he wants, he'll love reading the newspapers now. Maybe he'll come back, and maybe we can apprehend him. This is all I need—a Wolfman running around."

The chief, however, also warned anyone who saw the Wolfman not to try to catch him but to call the police immediately, according to the *Crescent-News*.

"We don't think it's a prank," Breckler told the *Blade*. "He's coming at people with a club in his hand. We think it's to the safety of our people to be concerned."

"WOLFMAN" HYSTERIA

In the days following the initial newspaper reports, werewolf hysteria ensued among some of the townspeople. The newspaper articles called the creature "the Wolfman," and the idea of an unidentified potential creature on the loose was frightening for many, especially those who lived near the railyard.

Nervous residents wanting protection from "the thing" quickly started calling police, according to the *Crescent-News*.

On August 3, a man called the police at 1:24 a.m. to report something had followed him on foot from Deatrick and South Clinton Streets to Hotel Henry (which later became the Valentine Theater and today houses a church) on Clinton Street, three blocks from the railyard.

"He indicated he didn't see anything but knew it was there because he had 'a crawly feeling up the back of his neck,'" the *Crescent-News* reported. "The report said the man was near hysteria and spent the remainder of the night in the lobby of the hotel."

Ten minutes later, a woman on the north side of town, which is the other end of town from the railyard, told police that a friend of hers had come to her house in near hysterics because she had read about "the thing" and

The railroad depot and yard where the Dogman of Defiance was spotted is still in use, although it doesn't have as much traffic as it did in the 1970s. *Kristina Smith*.

was "scared to death." The friend told the officers that at two o'clock each morning, something rattled her doorknob, the newspaper reported.

Then on August 4, another resident on the north side of town called the police to report that she heard something scratching at her door and that if anything came through the door, she would shoot it.

Other residents interviewed by the *Blade* weren't as concerned.

"It just doesn't sound like something that would happen in this neighborhood," Kathy Kehnast told the *Blade* on August 3. "This is probably the safest neighborhood around."

Fellow neighborhood resident Dale Ott said he let his kids play outside during the day and night and that he wasn't bothered by the Wolfman reports.

Rupert Figg, however, was a bit more concerned and ready to take on the creature, which he thought was more likely a person dressed as a werewolf.

"If I see him, the police are going to find out who he is," Figg said. "That's because they'll have to take him to the hospital to get the buckshot out."

Defiance resident Al Smith had moved to the city from Pennsylvania in February 1972 and worked for the *Crescent-News* at the time. He was on a different beat and didn't cover the story but remembers Ellen Armstrong, the city editor who wrote about the Dogman for the newspaper.

He recalls the staff discussing the case and questioning whether it was a hoax, but he doesn't remember Armstrong talking about it much. (Armstrong passed away a few years before work on this book began.)

"I thought it was strange and a little weird, because you don't expect something like that to appear no matter where you are," Smith said. "There were enough people who saw it. Why would you make up a story like this? With anything, you want to see proof."

Smith is very familiar with the area where the sightings occurred and sees how someone could have concealed themselves in the growth around the tracks and river.

"It's changed somewhat today, because it used to be more grown-up and brushy at that time," he said. "There used to be more train traffic there. There would be railcars that would be just sitting there."

For his part, Smith wasn't concerned for his safety. Although the newspaper's offices are just a few blocks from the railyard, his work shift didn't start until 7:00 a.m., hours after the Dogman sightings happened. He lived in an apartment complex on the north side of town, well away from the railyard, and was in the habit of locking his doors before the creature sightings started.

The werewolf mania continued for a few days, with unexplained sightings popping up in other northern Ohio towns.

About fifty miles northeast of Defiance in Toledo, John Szemansco, a twenty-two-year-old University of Toledo pharmacy student, reported that "what looked like a werewolf" darted in front of his car while he was driving on Sylvania Avenue near Talmage Road, according to an August 9 article in the *Blade*. He called police, who dismissed his report as a joke.

Sightings of hairy monsters were also reported in the city of Tiffin in Seneca County and in an unspecified location in Wyandot County, according to the *Blade*. Both counties neighbor each other and are located east of Defiance.

After that, the Dogman seemingly disappeared. On August 11, the *Crescent-News* answered a reader who asked whether the beast had been sighted. Police patrolled the area regularly but had not found the culprit, the paper reported.

"It was gone as quickly as it came," Smith said.

DEFIANCE FORGETS, BUT DOGMAN HAS PROMINENT PLACE IN FOLKLORE

After August 1972, the Dogman quickly began to fade from memory. Locals didn't talk about it much, and many who were around at that time don't remember it.

Several years ago, Kent and Janet McClary, who are part of a team that hosted the paranormal radio show *Dead Air* in Northwest Ohio for sixteen years, tracked down the police chief's wife in Florida. The chief had passed away, and his widow didn't remember anything about the Dogman story or her husband ever discussing it, they said.

Smith was the first person from Defiance they were able to locate who remembered the story. For years, they had been trying to find anyone from the town who recalled the phenomenon.

But it's not unusual for a story like Defiance's to fade, said Lyle Blackburn, a noted author of books about cryptid creature sightings, a producer of documentaries on cryptid creatures and a speaker and guest on various TV shows that on Discovery and the Travel Channel.

"Some of these can kind of be forgotten if there's no vehicle to keep promoting them," he said. "Say a movie had been made about this or there had been a local museum that had put an exhibit in there, then people would have remembered the Defiance werewolf more. As time went on, it just gets forgotten."

Other towns around the country with a cryptid creature story often celebrate it with festivals and souvenirs. For example, Point Pleasant, West Virginia, just over the Ohio border, has a Mothman Festival each year that draws cryptid enthusiasts from across the country.

The Dogman of Defiance story, however, had a resurgence in recent years thanks in part to the 2016 Dogman Symposium, organized by Ken Gerhard, a cryptozoologist and author. Blackburn was the master of ceremonies for the event, which took place in Defiance.

"The purpose was to explore the legends and sightings of what is known as Dogman that is a category of cryptid that resembles a werewolf," Blackburn said. "[Gerhard] was wanting to do that in a place that had some significance to the subject."

While whatever witnesses saw was dubbed the Wolfman or a werewolf at the time, it is known more commonly today as Dogman. Dogmen differ from werewolves; a Dogman is believed to be a bipedal, wolf-like creature, Blackburn explained. Werewolves are believed to be more traditional, supernatural monsters that transform from man to wolf.

Dogmen are mostly thought of as beasts with unknown origins and do not necessarily result from a human transformation. Many cryptozoology enthusiasts believe the Defiance creature is a Dogman instead of a werewolf.

The Dogman Symposium received media coverage, which brought the local story back to the public. The *Crescent-News* reported that attendees came from as far away as New York, Pennsylvania and Wisconsin.

In the following years, various media companies and groups with an interest in the subject have aired stories or posted videos and blogs about the Dogman on social media.

Regardless of how well the Dogman of Defiance is remembered, the story is unique among those of Dogmen and other cryptid legends because reliable sources documented it well, Blackburn said. It stands out from other Dogmen sightings, such as those in rural and desolate areas of Wisconsin and Michigan, because it happened in a more urban setting.

"You have newspaper articles that have documented the facts," he said. "You don't always have that in some cases."

The Dogman sightings also came during a sort of golden age for cryptids and monsters, Blackburn said. The Bermuda Triangle captured the public's imagination at the time. The Patterson-Gimlin film purporting to capture Bigfoot on film was released in 1967, and *The Legend of Boggy Creek*, a movie about sightings of a Bigfoot-type monster in Fouke, Arkansas, was released in 1972.

"Newspapers felt that that was something worth writing about because people were interested," he said. "Whereas now, these would be hard-pressed to get any space in the newspaper. It probably would end up in their blog, but it wouldn't get in the paper. It was definitely a trend in 1972."

There were other towns in the 1970s that had werewolf or Dogman sightings.

In 1971, Wolfman sightings were reported in Lawton, Oklahoma. Three teens ultimately confessed to being the culprits. They were just having some fun with a Halloween mask, the *Lawton Constitution* reported in March 1971. A werewolf-like creature was sighted and believed to have killed three dogs in June 1978 in Vidor, Texas, according to the *Orange Leader*, the local newspaper in Vidor.

In addition to its excellent documentation, the Defiance case stands out from others due to its pure bizarreness. Whatever was sighted was described by all witness as being hairy, even on its feet, but wearing jeans and carrying a stick or two-by-four.

"I don't recall any other cases, at least Dogman cases, where the creature was holding the weapon or anything," Blackburn said. "That's totally unique.…It sounds like a prank really, or somebody dressing up. Even that is totally bizarre. Why would somebody dress in not just a Wolfman mask?"

More than fifty years after the Dogman appeared and vanished, these questions remain unanswered.

"It seems only in Ohio would somebody dress up as a werewolf to try to scare a rail worker with a stick," Blackburn said. "It's just weird."

4

SOUTH BAY BESSIE

Shortly after midnight on a late March morning in 1912, Kelleys Island residents were jolted from their sleep by the sound of booming and crackling ice on the lake outside their cottages.

Half-dressed and likely throwing coats over their pajamas, some of the residents rushed outside toward the shoreline to see what could be causing such a ruckus.

Some used binoculars to try to pinpoint the source of the noise, and others built a fire on the shoreline to try to cast more light in the direction of the lake.

"Astounded at the phenomenon and utterly unable to account for it, the group, now increased to a score, watched the ice field," the *Sandusky Daily Register* reported on April 1, 1912. "Except for that one spot, the surface of the ice lay inert and calm in the pale light of the moon."

Perplexed, the group began to turn back toward their homes when a huge black object emerged from the ice, flinging cakes of ice into the air and causing them to crash deafeningly back into the lake.

In the moonlight, the islanders saw the black object had a large head and gaping mouth with a row of teeth.

"For a moment, after raising its head above the water, the animal was still," the newspaper reported. "Then it reared a long neck high into the air and raised a huge finlike flapper onto the ice, as though to draw itself out of the water. But the ice gave way like so much paper and the beast fell back into the vortex of thrashing waves it created."

South Bay Bessie sightings have been reported over the years in the Lake Erie Islands region, including around South Bass Island, pictured here. *Kristina Smith.*

The creature made another attempt to pull itself onto the ice, revealing its large tail, before falling back into the open water it had created.

"Frightened almost out of their wits, the few remaining watchers ran to their homes and in the darkness of the rooms awaited the oncoming of the beast," the newspaper reported. "The crackling of the ice was heard for about a quarter of an hour longer."

The next morning, the residents armed themselves, although the paper did not specify what they armed themselves with, and went out to find and kill the beast. They found the ice was broken up until about two hundred feet from shore, probably the closest the animal had come to breaching the island shore.

Their search for the creature, however, was fruitless.

"Old settlers are unable to account for the occurrence, though they repeat stories of a monster sea serpent once seen five miles off Cedar Point," the newspaper reported.

Many believe this group of terrified islanders witnessed the Lake Erie Monster, known today as South Bay Bessie. As the *Daily Register* alluded, it was not the first appearance of the monster—nor would it be the last.

For generations, sightings of the monster have been reported across the lake, from sightings in the Lake Erie Islands region, which includes Kelleys Island, a popular summer spot for seasonal residents and tourists, to the deeper waters of Lake Erie's Central and Eastern Basins and as far inland as the Huron River near Milan.

HISTORIC SIGHTINGS

Newspaper articles from the 1800s and early 1900s reference local talk about sightings of sea serpents in Lake Erie. In 1898, the *Sandusky Register* shared the story of two serpents being sighted near Point Pelee in Ontario, Canada, across Lake Erie from Port Clinton and the most southern point of Canada.

Adam Oper, described as Point Pelee's head fisherman and a local farmer, told the *Register* a chilling story of his encounter with the beast, which the newspaper reported on July 8 that year.

Earlier that week, Oper and some farmhands went out to work in his field of rye near the shore. The group noticed that some shocks of rye had been knocked over, as if a "cyclone" had gone through, the newspaper reported.

Then, in front of Oper, another shock tumbled.

"He picked up the capsheaf, and just then he heard a peculiar grating sound and the whole mass of rye began to move," the newspaper reported. "In the center, a horrible head with glistening eyes and darting tongue was slowly raised and gradually a long, writhing bluish-black body twisted itself from beneath the sheaves, reaching entirely around the fallen shock.... The poor man stood like a sphinx, immovable and unmoved, transfixed by the terrible sight that met his gaze. How long this lasted he does not know, though it seemed hours, though it was more likely but a few seconds."

Oper then turned and ran as fast as he could, followed by the sounds of the serpent gliding behind him through the sheaves of rye. After pursuing Oper for about half a mile, the serpent turned and headed toward the lake.

The farmhands witnessed all of this, according to the newspaper, and saw the serpent swim away into the lake. They estimated the creature was between twenty-five and thirty feet long and said it looked mostly like an ordinary snake.

After that incident, Oper decided he didn't need the rye crop and offered it to anyone interested. At least by the day the article was printed, there were no takers.

The following morning, a group of fishermen in the same area spotted another serpent on the lake. They estimated this one was one hundred feet long, according to the same article in the *Register*. The creature had become entangled in fishing nets and was thrashing madly to free itself. Frightened, the fishermen observed it and decided to stay away from it. When they returned the next day, the nets were destroyed, and the creature was gone.

The *Register* deemed both accounts to be reliable.

"It is probably not necessary to remark that this is not a fish story but a sea serpent story and a true one," the newspaper opined, and it went on to vouch for the character of those who reported witnessing it.

The monster emerged again several times in 1912. Three months after the Kelleys Island incident, the monster showed up on the Huron River in Milan with a hunger for meat.

South Bay Bessie. *Illustration by Kari Schultz.*

One of the city's former mayors, H.E. Loager, was fishing on the river and had just caught a large black bass when he noticed a groundhog swimming across the river, closely chased by a swimming dog that appeared to a type of shepherd breed, the *Sandusky Daily Register* reported on June 6, 1912.

At a point where the river was sixty feet wide, a serpent's huge head came out of the water, revealing part of a body studded with tentacles and horns. The serpent snapped up the groundhog and swallowed it.

"With another dip of his huge head he took up the dog with one mouthful, and although the fisherman was many feet away he distinctly heard the crushing of the bones as the two animals were devoured by the serpent," the newspaper reported.

The ginormous snake then whirled around in the water a few times, creating a wake of three-foot waves, Loager told the newspaper. Next, a large sycamore tree tumbled down and blocked mouth of the river, where it empties into Lake Erie.

"Loager states that after the tree had fallen he plainly saw the serpent making desperate efforts to do away with this mighty obstacle, which was between him and liberty, but he could not budge it, and is now an unwilling prisoner in Huron River," the newspaper reported.

Loager went on to tell the newspaper that armed parties of hunters were planning to find and kill the beast.

They weren't successful, according to a *Sandusky Register* article published a little more than a week later, on June 15, 1912. Instead, various hunting parties found the beast furiously lashing about in the waters with its "mighty tail."

Local farmer William Heckleman and his hired hand saw three dogs kill some of Heckleman's sheep and were hotly pursing them with clubs when the dogs escaped into the Huron River. The serpent then showed its "horned and tentacled head" and beat the pair trying to exact their revenge on the dogs, the newspaper reported. The men told the newspaper they heard the same crunching of bones that the fisherman had mentioned hearing earlier that month.

After that, the serpent sightings dwindled until another angler, Barney Baladin of Norwalk, reported capturing what he called the serpent's offspring in the lake near Milan, according to a *Sandusky Register* article published on June 27, 1912. The newspaper reported the creature attracted large crowds but indicated the reporter did not actually see it. No photograph was included with the story.

"As he is not very good at figuring the dimensions he could not say how large the reptile was, but he gives a good description of it, saying that it is half crab and half fish, there being not less than 10 or 12 long arms sticking out from the fat body," the newspaper reported.

The following July, the *Sandusky Star-Journal* published a story about another captured sea monster. This one could have been a sea lion or similar aquatic creature, according to the newspaper article, which was published on July 28, 1913.

J.W. Whitman of Port Clinton and his brother, Samuel Whitman of Marblehead, were fishing on Johnson's Island, a small island connected to the Marblehead Peninsula by a causeway that faces the Cedar Point amusement park in Sandusky.

From their net sprang a "large, brown monster," the *Star-Journal* reported. The men tried to get the animal back into the net, but it flopped out and swam away.

"I never saw anything like it before," J.W. Whitman told the newspaper. "It was about six feet long and covered with brownish hair. A log of spots run down its breast. Its head was something like that of a sea lion, and its tail, too, made me think that was what it was. But its feet was what had us guessing. I'll swear it had at least a dozen."

MODERN SIGHTINGS

The creature was again sighted and reportedly captured by two Cincinnati fishermen in July 1931 near Sandusky, according to the *Sandusky Register*. But it ended up being a python that was probably planted there by the men, who had recently become involved with a traveling carnival. The affair was most likely a hoax, the newspaper reported.

Decades passed with the occasional sighting here and there, but Lake Erie monster mania wouldn't have a resurgence until the 1990s. That's also when the monster got its most commonly known moniker: South Bay Bessie.

John Schaffner, the publisher of the *Beacon* weekly newspaper in Port Clinton, remembers the phenomenon starting when the *Put-in-Bay Gazette*, a monthly newspaper from South Bass Island, a home to the summer tourist town Put-in-Bay, published a photograph as part of an April Fool's Day joke in its April 1990 edition. The photograph was of a large log next to a dock, but the newspaper editors had some fun with it.

"There was this long, curving slimy thing that was next to the dock," Schaffner recalled. "[The editor] did an entire story about how this was some kind of eel that had come in during a nor'easter and got stuck in the dock and thrashed away and wrecked the dock."

Schaffner was friends with the *Gazette*'s publishers and asked if he could rerun the story for fun in his weekly paper. They agreed, and the tale blew up, becoming what one might call a viral story today.

Not long afterward, the *Beacon* began receiving calls about sightings. A woman and her friend went walking every morning on Catawba Island, a peninsula off Port Clinton, and swore they saw the same eel that was pictured in the *Gazette* and then the *Beacon*.

Schaffner Publications, which is the parent company of the *Beacon*, owned an outdoors magazine with a toll-free number that wasn't used much. Schaffner decided to turn that number into a hotline for Lake Erie monster sightings.

The stories came from across the lake, and they were often very similar.

There was a retired schoolteacher who was renting a cottage on Kelleys Island's east side. One morning, around six o'clock, she was sitting on the porch with a cup of coffee and looking out over the calm, serene lake water. She suddenly noticed a foul stench.

"She looked out in the lake. She said: 'I saw humps coming in and out of the water, like the Loch Ness Monster,'" Schaffner said. "She was as serious as a heart attack."

There was a call from a guy from Bucyrus, Ohio, who was out fishing on the lake. His story was nearly identical to the teacher's.

"Every time they see it, it's (A) absolutely calm, and (B) it smelled," Schaffner said. "There seemed to be some common denominators here. Every time I got a call, I did a little story."

The Associated Press covered the monster mania and sent the Lake Erie serpent stories across the wires. An AP article published on September 30, 1990, in the *Los Angeles Times* shared a sighting story from the Brickner family, who were fishing on the lake. They returned to East Harbor State Park in Marblehead and told rangers there they saw a large creature about one thousand feet from their boat.

The family members told the AP the animal was black and about thirty-five feet long with a snakelike head, and it was moving as fast as their boat.

"I told my son that I wanted to get a look at it," Harold Brickner told the AP. "My son said: 'No way, that thing is bigger than we are.' So we stayed where we were."

For Schaffner, the stories led to TV and radio stations coming out to feature the monster. A TV crew from Japan even paid a visit.

South Bay Bessie is embraced on the shores of Lake Erie. This artwork was hung temporarily at the Greater Cleveland Aquarium. *Diane Fenster*.

An artist turned this stranded log on the Portage River in Oak Harbor into South Bay Bessie. *Kristina Smith*.

A radio station in Toledo interviewed Schaffner, and not long after, he said, "I was called by every shock jock in the United States from Arizona to Colorado to California. That was their morning thing; they wanted to have a good time with the Lake Erie Monster."

Eventually, the story ended up in supermarket tabloid the *National Enquirer*.

By this time, Schaffner and his coworkers decided to continue the fun and give the creature a name, so the newspaper had a naming contest. Bruce Theobald of Port Clinton came up with the winning moniker.

"The Loch Ness Monster, this thing was kind of tied to, was Nessie," Schaffner said. "Everybody called her Nessie, that's when Bessie came in. That's how they got South Bay Bessie."

A student artist created a sketch of the monster, and the *Beacon* began running a "Where's Bessie" contest in the newspaper each week. After several years, the student copyrighted the image, which Schaffner no longer has, and the newspaper switched to its "Where's Wylie" contest that it still uses today. Wylie is the giant fiberglass fish that Port Clinton, known as the walleye capital of the world, drops from a cable at midnight each year on New Year's Eve.

Since the 1900s, the South Bay Bessie sightings have gone quiet. Yet there are those who believe that Bessie is still there, beneath the waters of Lake Erie.

Schaffner can't say whether Bessie is real.

"The people who I talked to, when they called in, they weren't joking," he said. "They really thought they saw something."

WHAT DID THESE WITNESSES SEE? COULD THE LAKE ERIE MONSTER BE REAL?

In early sightings, South Bay Bessie was described as sea serpent. In later sightings, including those in the early and late twentieth century, she was described similarly to the Loch Ness Monster, with fins and flippers.

Across the United States, lakes and rivers have their own sea monster legends. Lake Champlain, Vermont, has Champ. Lake Tahoe, California, has Tessie. Lake Michigan has the less-colorfully named Lake Michigan Monster. All of them tend to be depicted much like the Loch Ness Monster in Scotland, known as Nessie, perhaps the most famous sea monster in the world. Nessie is regularly shown as a plesiosaurus, an extinct aquatic dinosaur.

Ray Popik, curator of the Greater Cleveland Aquarium, rules out the possibility that there is a plesiosaurus or similar creature that somehow survived and is now roaming Lake Erie.

"Just the age the of the lakes wouldn't have even come close to overlapping appropriate time scales for that kind of stuff," he said. "At that time, the Great Lakes didn't exist. The great ice age made the Great Lakes, and the great ice age came eons after the dinosaurs were extinct."

Whether South Bay Bessie actually exists depends on how she is defined, Popik said. If Bessie is a big snake or unusually large fish, it's possible, but very unlikely, that she's out in Lake Erie, he said.

"I would lean toward no," he said. "It's very rare in modern times that we're finding a large megafauna predator. We're always finding new species in science. They are usually bacteria and plankton."

But there are some notable examples of larger fish species discovered in the past fifty to two hundred years. One is the coelacanth, a prehistoric-like, large, deep-sea-dwelling fish that looks a bit like a grouper with flipper-like appendages that was believed to be extinct. In the 1950s, a scientist found one in a fish market, and they are now found in oceans off the coasts India and Africa, Popik said.

"They're a fascinating example of we didn't think this existed, but there it is," he said. "Sure, there could be things out there."

A more likely explanation is that witnesses have seen logs—like the one the *Put-in-Bay Gazette* showed in its April Fools edition—debris or other animals that create the illusion of a sea monster.

"Then there's just the human mind and human eye playing tricks on us," Popik said. "There are your old classic mermaid stories from the 1500s and 1600s. That type of stuff holds over and carries on in the lake."

Witnesses also could have spotted a sturgeon, one of the oldest species of fish that also has a prehistoric look and historically grew to be ten to twelve feet long, Popik said. Sturgeon used to be so prevalent in Lake Erie and its tributaries in the 1800s that they were considered a nuisance and were fished just to be removed.

Today, sturgeon remain an endangered species in Ohio, but they are making a comeback, thanks to efforts of Ohio wildlife and conservation agencies, and have again been spotted in Lake Erie. Some sturgeon, believed to have come from the Detroit River in Michigan, have been spotted in the lake.

Tory Gabriel, an extension program leader and fisheries educator for Ohio State University's Ohio Sea Grant College Program and Stone Laboratory, confirms a potential explanation for South Bay Bessie involving sturgeon.

LARGEST FISH EVER CAUGHT IN LAKE ERIE

Lake Erie fishermen Alfred McKillips, Albert Kugler and Sylvester Dwelle proudly display the 180-pound sturgeon they caught on April 29, 1935, near Kelleys Island. *Rutherford B. Hayes Presidential Library and Museums, Charles E. Frohman Collection.*

A juvenile sturgeon is ready for release as part of Ohio's program to reintroduce populations of the endangered fish to Lake Erie and its tributaries. *Ohio Division of Wildlife.*

Sturgeon normally spawn in groups. Although they normally do this in rivers and streams and cobbly and rocky substrate, they could conceivably spawn in the reefs of the shallow Western Basin of Lake Erie, which stretches from Toledo to Sandusky, when their populations were larger and more prolific.

"I suppose if a couple of large sturgeon were spawning on a shallow reef, it could appear from a distance to be multiple humps," Gabriel said. "They also do jump, not necessarily as a spawning behavior, but I have seen them do it throughout the summer. It is not very serpent-like, more like a stiff board popping out and splashing down, but they can make quite a splash."

There are some other larger fish species in the lake, such as long-nosed gar, flathead catfish and muskellunge, but they likely are not large enough and do not have the behaviors that would cause them to be confused with a lake monster, Gabriel said.

Other critters that could possibly be mistaken for serpent-like humps from a distance or just at a glimpse include beavers, snapping turtles, muskrats, water or fox snakes and diving birds, including loons and cormorants, Gabriel said.

He agrees that debris and large waterlogged trees could be mistaken for the monster, especially on a day with wind and waves or if the debris is caught on a reef and bobs up and down.

"It might be a stretch, but in the exact right conditions and areas, I could see that being as likely an explanation as anything listed [previously]," Gabriel said.

Whether South Bay Bessie is a sturgeon, a group of bobbing debris or an actual unidentified large predator, Ohio's North Coast has embraced the legend and had fun with it.

The Greater Cleveland Aquarium featured a large poster of a South Bay Bessie postcard in its Native Ohio Gallery, an area that features native Ohio species of fish and turtles and educates visitors about the species in their own backyard.

The Great Lakes Brewing Company in Cleveland proudly makes a Lake Erie Monster IPA, which has a green sea serpent on its label.

The Cleveland Monsters minor-league hockey team features a sea monster in its logo, and they were once known as the Lake Erie Monsters.

And those are just a few examples.

Even if she is a mythical creature in Lake Erie, South Bay Bessie at least exists in spirit, Popik said.

5

THE MELON HEADS OF KIRTLAND

One of the Buckeye State's more unusual urban legends comes from Lake County, a thirty-mile-long strip along Lake Erie's coast. It is in this scenic locale that a group of creatures known as "Melon Heads" (some literature uses the alternative "Melonheads") are said to terrorize the woods outside the town of Kirtland, which lies about a half hour's drive east of Cleveland.

The legend of the Melon Heads began at some point in the latter half of the twentieth century. Some versions place its events in the years immediately following World War II, while others claim it happened as late as the 1970s. Regardless, the legend of the Melon Heads reads like the mad scientist films that would have been popular in either era. It says the Melon Heads were the diabolical creation of a mysterious Dr. Crow. (At this point, we should pause to acknowledge the diversity within this piece of folklore. Depending on who is telling the story, its chief villain could be Dr. Kroh, Dr. Krow, Dr. Krowe, Dr. Crow or Dr. Crowe, and sometimes, the "doctor" goes unnamed. The surname "Crow" seems to be the most common in literature on the legend, so that is what this chapter will use.)

Crow and his wife are said to have been well-to-do socialites who moved into a small mansion on Wisner Road, which winds back and forth as it follows the Chagrin River. Dr. Crow was a physician, while Mrs. Crow worked with charities, helping children with disabilities.

The pair began adopting some of the orphaned children they worked with who suffered from a condition known as hydrocephalus, an excessive buildup of fluid in the brain. While this seems altruistic on the surface, the

Crows were hiding a horrible secret. Dr. Crow began using the adopted children as his personal science projects. He had developed a serum, which he tested on the children; it caused their brains and craniums to expand to monstrous proportions. Since they had veiny, bulbous heads reminiscent of the Talosians in the 1966 pilot of *Star Trek*, Crow hid his experiments from the nosy locals in Kirtland by imprisoning them in his estate.

One core tenet of the legend of the Melon Heads is that some kind of accident occurred that released Crow's test subjects into the woods of Lake County. In some versions, Mrs. Crow was somehow unaware of her husband's research on her adopted children and threatened divorce when she discovered the horrors happening in her own home. When Dr. Crow hit his wife, the deformed children became enraged and murdered the doctor, knocking a lamp over in the process. A fire quickly spread through the entire house, killing the Crows, the children and all evidence of the doctor's experiments.

Supposedly, when authorities arrived to investigate the scene, all they found was a burnt-out shell and several deformed skeletons, leaving them with a lot of questions. The fire on Wisner Road remained an unsolved mystery until locals began having unusual experiences in the years that followed. Drivers spoke of savage, child-size creatures with gigantic, melon-shaped heads that would chase their cars through the woods near Kirtland. Frightened farmers started locking up their animals after one of the humanoids was seen eating a dog. The Melon Heads, so the legend goes, have been stalking Lake County ever since.

This tale is only one of many arcs this legend has taken over the years. In a perhaps more fanciful telling, the Melon Heads are the result of illegal human research by the government. Sometimes, Dr. Crow's activities are situated within the context of this secret program, which was sheltered away from public view in rural northeastern Ohio. When a couple of Melon Heads escaped and were spotted by locals, the government decided to shut down the project and burned the lab to the ground. However, a handful of test subjects remained elusive, despite the best efforts of the unspecified agency to clean up any loose ends. These monstrosities are said to have survived through inbreeding in the backwoods of Lake County and still stalk those who venture into their territory.

There also exists an appalling, more supernatural version of this story that doesn't result in a race of escaped hybrids stalking Lake County. In this case, Dr. Crow was an illegal abortionist working out of his cabin in the woods outside Kirtland. Dr. Crow seems to simply exit this story without explanation, but the Melon Heads people report are explained as ghosts of the unborn who haunt the region, seeking vengeance against Crow.

The legend of the Melon Heads is incredibly malleable. Any of the details in the aforementioned accounts can be (and have been) interchanged with others. Some even include additional flourishes, in which the Melon Heads can only stagger their way through the woods, the victims of lobotomies from Dr. Crow, or they display superhuman speed and aggression due to genetic engineering.

How and when this legend emerged in Northeast Ohio is a bit of a mystery. For starters, the legend of the Melon Heads is not specific to Ohio. This urban legend also exists in southwestern Connecticut and western Michigan, with the Melon Heads from Connecticut being the most profiled in paranormal literature.

According to the New England Historical Society, people first began sharing Melon Head stories around Monroe, Connecticut, in the years after World War II. These Melon Heads share in New England's association with witchcraft and are said to be the products of satanic rituals or the inbred descendants of accused witches who were exiled to live in the woods. Some Connecticut versions opt for a more modern origin, with the Melon Heads being escaped cannibals from a burned-down insane asylum.

Melon Head stories from around Saugatuck Dunes State Park in Michigan also follow the asylum route but include the familiar doctor character. Here, a scientist was experimenting on the asylum's patients, who eventually escaped and turned to cannibalism when the building was burned down.

Historians and folklorists have attempted to find some basis for the legend of the Melon Heads but have mostly come up empty. The Connecticut Melon Heads have been associated with the Fairfield Hills Hospital, an actual psychiatric hospital that was abandoned in 1995. While Fairfield did have a reputation for experimenting on patients, including unnecessary lobotomies, no one has found evidence of the practices described in the legend. In Michigan, local historians have dismissed the idea that an asylum ever burned down around Saugatuck; however, there was a prison in the region that could have become conflated with an asylum in the legend.

The Ohio version of the legend of the Melon Heads has one unique feature: Dr. Crow. This character almost always plays a central role in the legend as it's told in Lake County. This has led some researchers to wonder if the name might be a clue into the legend's origins. Speaking with *Cleveland Magazine* in 2019, Bonnie Snyder, the director of the Lake County Genealogy Society, said that she had been unable to find a Dr. Crow (or any alternative spellings) in the U.S. census or in the society's obituary records.

There are, however, three area doctors who appear in historic newspapers whose names could have been co-opted by the legend. In nearby Hubbard,

Ohio, Dr. Thomas Crowe served as a city council member in the 1970s and 1980s. Looking at Kirtland, specifically, there was a Dr. John Kroh who worked as a veterinarian at the Kirtland Animal Hospital in the early 1970s.

But perhaps most interesting is Dr. Dean Kroh, a physician and surgeon from Pennsylvania who served as a missionary with the Christian and Missionary Alliance from the 1950s through the 1980s. During his time working in central Africa and later Cambodia, Kroh provided much-needed medical care to thousands of sick and injured locals, including children. Whenever Kroh returned to the United States, he often spoke at Alliance churches throughout Pennsylvania and eastern Ohio, and stories about his missionary work appeared in several newspapers in the area.

It is important to emphasize that there is nothing to suggest these doctors did anything like what is described in the legend of the Melon Heads. This research is only speculation on where early storytellers may have acquired the name "Crow" or "Kroh."

The association of the term *melon head* with this urban legend is an interesting one. On its surface, it seems like a straightforward way to describe how these beings supposedly look with their bulbous heads. But historians and folklorists suspect the use of this name may reveal some cultural anxieties embedded in the legend.

The term *melon head* first emerged sometime in the 1800s to describe an idiotic or foolish person. It became a popular insult in everyday vernacular in the post–World War II years. For example, in 1948, the *Hartford Courant* reported on a rash of people who were shooting electric transformers with rifles and described the perpetrators as "melon-heads." The next year, the *Cincinnati Enquirer* began carrying an educational comic strip on traffic safety starring Mr. Melonhead, who taught new drivers what not to do on the road. The term naturally found room in politics, and the *Herald Press* of St. Joseph, Michigan, published a satirical comic strip called "Candidate Melonhead" throughout the 1964 presidential campaign.

Taken literally, the term was also used to physically describe men who were losing their hair, and a handful of bald men embraced the title by forming the Club of the Melon Heads in Portugal in 1965.

This idea of a melon head being a stupid and backward person has led some folklorists to consider the Melon Heads of Kirtland and elsewhere as the embodiment of something else. "Melon Head stories surfaced in Connecticut after World War II, a time when people moved away from cities into the suburbs. They probably reflect the New York exurbanite's prejudice and fear of isolated rural folk," writes the New England Historical

Melonhead. *Illustration by Kari Schultz.*

Society. The New England Historical Society goes on to speculate that there may also be a connection between the depiction of the Melon Heads as malformed, backward "others" and the similar-sounding Melungeons, a small nineteenth-century ethnic group from the Appalachian regions of eastern Tennessee and Kentucky. The Melungeons were known to have an ancestry that included European immigrants, freed formerly enslaved people and Natives. This group is believed to have been singled out and ostracized by surrounding Appalachian communities due to their poverty and mixed-race status, although historians debate to what extent this marginalization actually occurred.

Many local historians and paranormal writers have presented a more mundane explanation for where the legend of the hydrocephalic Melon Heads originated. As Kit Lane, a historian from Saugatuck, Michigan, explained to the *Detroit Free Press* in 2011, "The lore probably spun from encounters with a child with hydrocephalus who lived in the area decades ago." Authors Andrew Henderson, James Willis and Loren Coleman suggest in their book *Weird Ohio* that a similarly misunderstood child possibly spawned the Kirtland legend: "Some say there was at one time a family with a mentally disabled child with an oversized cranium who used to stand at the fence at the edge of his parents' property and that all the myths and horror stories are much ado about one unfortunate kid."

While the idea of locals spinning yarns based on a child's medical condition certainly seems plausible, the fact that this explanation occurs in multiple tellings in various locations seems to indicate that this "child with hydrocephalus" is also part of the legend's mythos.

The association of the Melon Heads with hydrocephalus is misrepresentative at best and offensive at worst. Hydrocephalus is a much more common and less dramatic condition than this legend of these ghoulish figures would lead one to believe. According to Johns Hopkins, hydrocephalus "is the accumulation of too much cerebrospinal fluid inside the ventricles when the normal production and absorption of cerebrospinal fluid is disrupted." Cerebrospinal fluid is an essential fluid produced by the brain and circulated throughout the nervous system. In most people, this fluid is produced and disposed of at a similar rate, but certain medical conditions can lead to an excess or deficit of cerebrospinal fluid surrounding the brain.

The Hydrocephalus Association reports that some 1 million Americans are affected by hydrocephalus. While the condition does appear in adults, especially as the result of a traumatic brain injury, it is most often seen in pediatric cases. Approximately 1 out of every 770 babies develops hydrocephalus in early childhood, and it is roughly as common as Down syndrome. The condition can have numerous causes, and its treatment usually requires several brain surgeries throughout childhood to install shunts to drain excess fluid.

Hydrocephalus can, in fact, lead to an enlargement of the cranium. However, unlike the cartoonishly bulbous swelling seen in the heads of the Melon Heads, the swelling hydrocephalus causes is often too subtle to be seen with the naked eye. Cranial abnormalities are sometimes visible during infancy and early childhood, but they usually disappear as the child grows. While hydrocephalus can and does contribute to several behavioral, developmental and memory disorders, most people diagnosed with hydrocephalus go on to lead full and independent lives. The savage and cannibalistic behavior of the Melon Heads is a grotesque parody of a serious medical condition that perhaps ought to be reconsidered.

This inappropriate association with hydrocephalus notwithstanding, the legend of the Melon Heads has become a harmless rite of passage in Lake County for several decades. Teenagers and thrill seekers drive into the woods near Kirtland to go "Melon Head hunting" in the hopes of seeing something strange and getting a good scare. In *Weird Ohio*, one Kirtland resident identified as "Paul" recalled that in 1964, he and his friends were caught hunting for the Melon Heads by the local police. Unfortunately, the only unexpected thing they saw was the inside of the police station, where they were told to call their parents. The pastime even has its own Facebook page titled "Melonhead Hunting in Kirtland Ohio," where locals share their experiences and organize hunts, although interest in the group appears to have waned in recent years.

The monstrous nature of the Melon Heads has provided inspiration for local filmmakers in the horror genre. In 2010, Brian C. Lawlor wrote and directed *Legend of the Melonheads*. The short film, which has a runtime of about an hour, blends the Melon Head story with several other local legends, such as those of Crybaby Bridge and Gravity Hill, common pieces of folklore found in towns across the country. A similar short film based on the Michigan version of the Melon Head legend was released in 2011.

The legend of the Melon Heads is certainly a bizarre one, even by the standards of cryptozoology. It successfully combines weirdness, conspiracy theories and people's morbid curiosity in order to create staying power in a diverse set of places. This legend provides a good case study in just how flexible folklore can be when its details shift to fit a new environment.

6

MOTHMAN

P oint Pleasant, West Virginia, is a small community that, in the words of one unnamed 1810 traveler, is "pleasantly situated immediately above the mouth of the Great Kanawha, on an extensive and fertile bottom of the Ohio, of which it has a fine prospect up and down that river."

Once the site of a British colonial fort, the town was slow to thrive in the years following the American Revolution. The nineteenth-century historian Virgil A. Lewis wrote that the townsfolk had come to believe in a "superstition that because of the fiendish murder of [the Shawnee Chief] Cornstalk there in 1777 [during Lord Dunmore's War], the place was laid under a curse for a hundred years."

During World War II, the army built the West Virginia Ordnance Works, an eight thousand acre complex located about five miles north of Point Pleasant that manufactured explosives and ammunition. The factory stored the weapons it produced in dozens of dome-shaped bunkers known as "igloos." The plant, which employed thousands of workers, closed at the end of the war. Despite losing its leading employer, the industrial river town continued to reap the benefits of the nation's postwar boom well into the 1960s.

Portions of the abandoned site became a landfill, while another 3,600 acres of it became the Clifton F. McClintic Wildlife Management Area, which locals took to calling the "TNT Area." On November 15, 1966, two Point Pleasant couples not only ventured into the overgrown TNT Area but also stumbled into Ohio and West Virginia history.

THE PARADISE TOWN THAT HAD A VISIT FROM HELL

IN FEAR OF THE UFO-BIRD

Is the dreaded mothman poised to strike again?

| THE HAUNT | LONNIE McDANIEL stands outside powerhouse where Mothman was frequently spotted. Star's reporter found it eerily cold. | THE MONSTER | ROGER Scarberry's eyewitness sketch of Mothman, verified by others. |

Artist's rendition of Roger Scarberry's original sketch of Mothman. *From the* San Antonio Express, *February 16, 1975.*

That night, a Tuesday, was a cold one, with temperatures dipping into the thirties. Roger and Linda Scarberry and their friends Steve and Mary Mallette, all newly married and in their late teens or early twenties, decided to drive up to the old factory just before midnight.

It was never established at the time exactly what the Scarberrys and Mallettes were doing in the TNT Area so late, leading to speculation that they had driven up there to drink or take drugs. The couples had to tell reporters multiple times that they were not under the influence of any drugs or alcohol. In a 2001 interview with Donnie Sergent for his website Mothmanlives.com, Linda Scarberry (since remarried and with a new last name) reiterated, "Absolutely not. No one in the car at the time of sighting was drinking or using drugs of any kind....We were just out chasing parkers."

As they drove near the power plant for the old factory, they spotted a winged humanoid creature that was, as they described it to the *Point Pleasant Register* the following day, "about six or seven feet tall, having a wingspan of 10 feet and red eyes about two inches in diameter and six inches apart." The two couples, who were "slightly pale and tired from lack of sleep" when they spoke with reporters, went on to liken what they saw to a "man with wings" or "maybe what you would visualize as an angel" that was light gray in color with "eyes, which glowed red, only when their lights shined on it."

The Scarberrys and the Mallettes said they saw the creature multiple times throughout the night. After Roger Scarberry turned the car around and began driving south along Route 62 toward Point Pleasant, the "man-sized bird," as the *Register* called it, appeared in front of their vehicle again. This time, it took to the air, "straight up, like a helicopter," and gave chase. "I was doing 100–105 mph and it was just gliding over top, sorta moving from side to side," Scarberry told the United Press International (UPI) newswire. "You could hear a flapping noise, then it came down at the car, making a squealing noise like a mouse."

The thing seemed to have an aversion to light, and the couples said it abandoned the pursuit when they came to a lit area near the farm of C.C. Lewis. However, according to the Ohio newspaper the *Athens Messenger*, when they left the refuge of the farm, they spotted it yet again, this time standing near the carcass of a dead dog on the side of the road.

When they finally reached town, the four found Mason County Sheriff's Deputy Millard Halstead and convinced him to go with them to the TNT Area. Along the way to the plant, they discovered the remains of the dog had disappeared. They spotted movement in the shadows once they arrived at the power plant, and Halstead shined his spotlight to see wisps of dust in a cornfield, but he did not report seeing the creature directly.

Steve Mallette theorized that the thing had taken up residence in the plant and was living in one of its boilers. "This doesn't have an explanation to it," he told the *Register*. "It was an animal but nothing like I've seen before." Despite the sleepless night, Mallette stated they still intended to go looking for it later that afternoon, and he later said he found the creature crawling inside one of the boilers when they returned.

Word started to spread throughout the region on Wednesday. Mary Hyre, a trusted longtime correspondent for the *Messenger* who was living in Point Pleasant, began providing nearly daily coverage of the bizarre story, and a staff writer for the UPI wire service arrived in town whose reporting would turn the "Mason County Monster" into a national curiosity by that Thursday.

The Mason County Sheriff's Department received several calls that Wednesday night from people who claimed they had seen the "bird." Four teens said it appeared to them in the yard of Ralph Thomas, who lived just northeast of the TNT Area, where it stared at them briefly before flying off. An Ohioan who asked not to be identified claimed he was in Gallipolis, directly across the Ohio River from Point Pleasant, when "it" chased him.

One particularly interesting report came from Doddridge County, West Virginia, nearly ninety miles away. Newell Partridge said he spotted a similar creature with "red reflectors" for eyes on his farm at about 10:30 p.m. on Tuesday night, nearly two hours before the Scarberrys and Mallettes said they saw the bird. Partridge said that when he opened his door, his growling German shepherd took off after the thing, never to return.

Writing under the headline "Another Reports 'Bird Creature': Doddridge Incidents Related?" UPI connected Partridge's dognapped German shepherd to the dead dog the Scarberrys and Mallettes had seen near the Lewis farm. From the available documents, Partridge did not report his dog's disappearance until after he would have read about the Scarberry-Mallette sighting in the news. The prevailing assumption in Mothman literature is that the monster killed the dog and flew its meal to Point Pleasant. The editor of the *Register* alluded to this early on by working out the math on how long it would take the creature to travel that distance given its reported flight speed.

The rest of the week was such a frenzy that some wondered if Point Pleasant Mayor D.B. Morgan could have orchestrated the bird as a stunt to promote a new bird sanctuary in the area. "Every intersection was jammed with parked cars and small clumps of laughing, jostling young adults," wrote Hyre for the *Messenger*. "Huge abandoned powder plant buildings rang with shrieks of youngsters." The Point Pleasant Police Department estimated that more than one thousand people went into the TNT Area that Thursday night, and they were alarmed that the disorganized posse wandering around in the dark was armed. Officers said that most of the groups they saw had "at least one gun," and on one occasion, they even heard an automatic rifle ring out.

The authorities had other concerns beyond public safety. Dr. Robert L. Smith, a professor of wildlife biology at West Virginia University, met with Mason County Sheriff George Johnson on Friday. He warned the sheriff that the creature people were seeing was most likely protected by a federal wildlife law, the Migratory Bird Treaty Act of 1918, and that even the misdemeanor offenses outlined in the law could result in a hefty fine and prison time.

Smith said the descriptions of the bird perfectly matched those of a sandhill crane, a large, gray bird that can stand up to five feet tall and have a seven-foot wingspan. The species is most easily identified by the bright red skin around its eyes. "Somebody who has never seen anything like it before could easily get the impression it is a flying man." Smith told the *Huntington Herald-Dispatch.* "Car lights would cause the bare skin to reflect as big red circles around the eyes." While sandhill cranes don't usually travel as far east as West Virginia during their winter migration from central Canada to Mexico and the Gulf Coast, the biologist said it wasn't unheard of.

By the weekend, Sheriff Johnson had heard enough. He issued a statement warning locals not to harm the bird and that his men would arrest anyone caught in the TNT Area with a loaded firearm after dark.

The name "Mothman" appeared in print within two days of the incident, when the Associated Press (AP) picked up the story on November 17: "Holy Moth Man! Once they said flying saucers came out the sky near here—now it's a flying man." Still, locals continued to refer to the creature as the bird for some time.

Over the next several days, the surrounding towns had fun speculating what the Mothman could be. Students from a high school science club in Proctorville, an Ohio town about forty miles downriver from Point Pleasant, tried to claim responsibility. Their teacher told the *Messenger* they had released two large weather balloons and that "imagination" had done the rest. Leading with headlines like "Don't Peck on Bird—He's a Tough Hombre" and "It's a Moth! It's a Plane! No—It's a Sandhill Crane," editors for city papers seemed to enjoy the idea of rural Appalachian "hill people" panicking over a bird.

But the Scarberrys and Mallettes had planted their flag on the issue and told the *Register* they remained convinced that whatever they saw, it wasn't a crane. For that resolve, they endured substantial ridicule. During her 2001 interview, Linda Scarberry was the only original witness willing to talk with Mothmanlives.com, but she still requested her new married name be kept private. "The only people who haven't made fun of us is you, John Keel, Mary Hyre, and [paranormal documentarian] Dan Draslin."

With a growing consensus that there probably wasn't a monster on the loose, the crowds began to depart shortly after Sheriff Johnson issued his warning. "'Mothman' Mystery Fades with Expert Explanation," the AP proclaimed. By month's end, the spectacle was over.

It looked as if Mothman was on its way to obscurity as a quirky local legend. The *Register* returned to covering Point Pleasant's routine news. But the local gumshoe Mary Hyre continued to meticulously track Mothman sightings for the *Messenger*. In December, she published a curious article not about the bird but about several unidentified flying objects that were seen just across the river in Ohio. The last paragraph reveals why she had suddenly taken an interest in flying saucers. Some prominent names from the UFO movement, a niche group in the 1960s, were in town asking all kinds of weird questions. Two of these UFO researchers, Gray Barker and John Keel, would turn Mothman into one of the most famous monster legends in American history.

Gray Barker was a native West Virginian, born in 1925, whose influence on the burgeoning field of ufology in the mid-twentieth century is difficult to understate. While working as a theater promoter in the 1950s, the former English major began collecting stories from people who claimed to see flying saucers and "little green men." He got his start as a paranormal writer by compiling supposed witness accounts of the Flatwoods Monster, another well-known West Virginia cryptid with UFO connections, into an absorbing article for Raymond Palmer's *FATE Magazine* in 1953. Palmer is best remembered as the editor of *Amazing Stories*, the influential science-fiction short story magazine credited with popularizing the genre in the 1930s and 1940s. But he launched *FATE* as "the world's leading magazine of the paranormal" in 1948.

Barker's article "The Monster and the Saucer" launched his full-time career writing science-fiction as well as stories about allegedly real supernatural phenomena. He eventually became a leading publisher in the field himself by launching his own magazine, the *Saucerian Bulletin*, as well as a book press, Saucerian Publications.

Barker forever changed UFO lore when he published *They Knew Too Much About Flying Saucers* in 1956. The best-selling book described the unsettling experience of one of Barker's former publishers, Albert K. Bender, who, in 1953, had mysteriously shut down his civilian UFO research group, the International Flying Saucer Bureau, as well as his magazine *Space Review*. The reason for Bender's sudden aboutface on UFO research, according to Barker, was that three terrifying men in black suits had warned him to stop looking into flying saucers. In Barker's telling, these "Men in Black" traveled in groups of three, drove black Cadillacs and behaved in a strange, seemingly inhuman manner.

The Men in Black concept introduced a captivating cloak-and-dagger element into the UFO mystery. Were these dark figures government agents engaged in a UFO cover-up? Did they come from some shadowy secret organization working with the aliens? Ufologists eagerly began collecting other stories about the infamous Men in Black, even some purported to predate Bender's experience. Barker and Bender published a sequel of sorts in 1962 titled *Flying Saucers and the Three Men*, which speculated that the Men in Black were, in fact, extraterrestrials.

Barker's visits to Point Pleasant in the wake of the Mothman sightings culminated in *The Silver Bridge*, which he published in 1970. The book was not widely read at the time, and its copies were hard to come by until a second edition was released in 2002.

As a strict chronicle of what happened in Point Pleasant, *The Silver Bridge* largely falls short. Barker was a gifted writer, and he used lively, literary prose to embellish the accounts witnesses gave him into a captivating story. In fact, some anecdotes in *The Silver Bridge* are completely fictitious. In "Gray Barker: My Friend, the Myth-Maker," published in *Skeptical Inquirer* in 1998, Barker's protégé John C. Sherwood quotes a letter he received from Barker regarding *The Silver Bridge*: "About half of it is recounting actual sightings and events in the Ohio Valley circa 1966.…I think that the 'true accounts' are told in an exciting way, but I have deliberately stuck in fictional chapters based roughly on cases I had heard about."

Barker had a reputation for skewing facts in favor of entertainment. According to Sherwood, Barker once asked him to rewrite a science-fiction short story he had submitted as if it was fact. Barker published Sherwood's rewritten piece as "Flying Saucers: Time Machines? by Dr. Richard Pratt" in *Saucer News* in 1969. Barker later used the protagonist from Sherwood's story, Dr. Pratt, in his 1983 book *M.I.B: The Secret Terror Among Us*, again presenting the "doctor" as a real person. One vocal critic of paranormalism, journalist Jason Colavito, has gone so far as to call Barker "a UFO skeptic who wrote, to be blunt, lies and hoaxes for cash."

While Barker's legacy remains controversial, it is undeniable that he did the same thing for the Mothman mythos that he had done for the Men in Black. *The Silver Bridge* was the first work to draw together several disparate anecdotes into a commonly accepted canon that continues to make up the Mothman legend.

Two weeks before the first Mothman sightings, newspapers and television networks across the country covered the experience of a West Virginia salesman named Woodrow "Woody" Derenberger, who claimed that he had been stopped by an alien craft on Interstate 77 on his way home from Marietta, Ohio. Derenberger said a "spaceman," who identified himself as "Cold," exited the craft, walked to his truck and engaged him in a friendly telepathic chat.

Barker includes Derenberger's tale early in *The Silver Bridge*, and in a later chapter, it is told from the point of view of the spaceman, now referred to as "Indrid Cold." (It is unclear precisely when the alien gained a first name.) It is never explained how the Derenberger-Cold affair relates to Mothman, but Barker's inclusion of the story implies that all the strange phenomena reported in the area in late 1966 should be considered connected.

Barker likewise wrote chapters featuring the Men in Black and the Curse of Cornstalk. In his novelistic style, he relays accounts of odd, black-suited men harassing UFO witnesses. He poetically speculates that all of the strange happenings could be the dramatic culmination of Point Pleasant's fabled curse stemming from its betrayal of Chief Cornstalk during its origins as a British fort. However, the hundred-year malediction mentioned by the historian Virgil Lewis in 1892, which should have expired in 1877, seems to have been extended by Barker to two hundred years to cover the 1960s.

The most crucial contribution of Barker to the Mothman legend relates to the title of his book. Around 5:00 p.m. on December 15, 1967, an ominous thirteen months to the day after the first Mothman sighting, the Silver Bridge, which had connected Point Pleasant to Gallipolis for nearly forty years, collapsed in a matter of seconds during rush hour traffic. According to the West Virginia Department of Transportation, witnesses recalled hearing a "loud gunshot-like noise" and then watching the bridge fold "like a deck of cards." First responders braved frigid waters in a vain effort to rescue survivors. Ultimately, the disaster claimed the lives of forty-six people, many of whom lived in Point Pleasant.

In the aftermath of the collapse, President Lyndon B. Johnson ordered the creation of the Presidential Task Force on Bridge Safety "to begin immediately an intensive study of the Ohio River bridge tragedy and to conduct a national survey of bridge safety." The resulting investigation prompted Congress to pass national safety standards for highway bridges in 1968.

It's also worth noting that Mothman and UFOs disappeared from the *Register* in the months following the Silver Bridge Collapse. There's no doubt that publishing stories about monsters and extraterrestrials in light of such a tragedy would appear to be in poor taste. Writing three years after the incident, Barker never explains how Mothman connects with the disaster, but by closing his book with a sighting that occurred just after the bridge collapse, he implies an intangible association between the two.

Whereas Barker is not well known outside of ufology, anyone who has heard of Mothman likely knows the name of Barker's contemporary John Keel. Keel was a freelance writer in his mid-thirties when he arrived in Point

HUGE CRANE HAULS VEHICLE FROM RIVER NEAR GALLIPOLIS
Two Bodies Were Found in Car That Fell as Bridge Collapsed—AP

Recovery efforts following the collapse of the Silver Bridge on December 15, 1967. *From the* Dayton Daily News, *December 18, 1967.*

Pleasant. He published his first work in a science-fiction magazine when he was sixteen years old and decided a writing career would be his life's pursuit. Keel subscribed to the ideas of Charles Fort, an early twentieth-century writer who collected newspaper reports on strange phenomena and has been called by one of his biographers the "man who invented the supernatural." Keel identified himself as a "Fortean" and traveled the world researching topics like magick, yetis and flying saucers for such paranormal publications as *Flying Saucer Review* and *Saucer News.* Over the course of his life, Keel published over fifteen books.

Keel was in Washington, D.C., trying to get the U.S. Air Force to divulge the whereabouts of Project Blue Book's records when Barker called him from Point Pleasant to tell him about the bird. While the two shared the UFO publishing space, they were more often competitors than collaborators. Keel arrived on December 7 and immediately got to work. He interviewed the Scarberrys, the Mallettes, the Thomases and the local sheriff's deputies and had them take him to the TNT Area. He also visited Mary Hyre's office to see what reports she had been receiving.

Yes, Keel was intrigued by sightings of Mothman and UFOs, but he was especially interested in hearing what people had to say about the MIB, an abbreviation for the Men in Black he coined himself. Residents told him that "dark tan" individuals driving black limousines and claiming to be "census takers" were showing up on the porches of Mothman witnesses to ask for personal information. Mothman witness Marcella Bennett claimed a black Ford Galaxy had tried to force her off the road in December. Just after the new year in 1967, Mary Hyre wrote Keel to tell him about a small man, less than five feet tall and wearing a short-sleeve shirt on a twenty-degree day, who barged into her office to ask for directions because his car had stalled and "he had hitchhiked all the way from Detroit." She said he stood in front of her desk as if frozen and leered at her uncomfortably.

Keel returned to Point Pleasant sporadically during what he called "the year of the Garuda [a mythical winged humanoid being from the Hindu tradition]" and built a friendship with Hyre, who kept him supplied with a steady stream of weird reports. As the year progressed, Keel brought the *Messenger* reporter evermore into his world, and she made UFOs a regular feature of her column "Where the Waters Mingle." On March 15, she described her own sighting of a UFO after she "parked in front of the State Theater and along with others watched it travel very slowly southward. There were no sounds."

In a letter to Hyre dated November 3, 1967, preserved digitally on the website JohnKeel.com, Keel can be seen encouraging Hyre to become an active participant in helping him foil the MIB:

> *I urge you to follow my example. Act interested and get people to talk about what they have seen but do not try to give them any clues....Don't let people know that you have heard of these odd characters before. The best plan for you to follow is to write only about the UFOs, not about the "people." Play up an occasional monster story however, because they probably expect these monsters to receive some publicity. If there is an open contact in your area and the witness comes to you freely with the story, I would appreciate if you would check with me before printing the story. "They" might be trying to get some more lies into circulation. Or they might be setting up some kind of hoax. Things are terribly complicated now.*

By the time Keel published his best-selling book *The Mothman Prophecies* in 1975, he had already been writing about Mothman for years. He dedicated a chapter to it in his 1970 encyclopedic book, *Strange Creatures from Time and Space*, in which he details twenty-six Mothman sightings prior to the Silver Bridge collapse. But *The Mothman Prophecies* was intended to serve as his thorough, boots-on-the-ground report of everything that supposedly happened in Point Pleasant.

Following the framework established by Barker in *The Silver Bridge*, Keel mentions the Woodrow Derenberger story early on and then concludes with the bridge disaster. Keel filled the pages in between with not only the familiar Mothman encounters but also flying saucer reports going back to the nineteenth century, ancient tales of winged creatures from around the world, all sorts of alleged ET contactee stories, hauntings and poltergeists as well as Keel's interactions with the Air Force.

At first glance, the organization of Keel's thoughts in *The Mothman Prophecies* can seem almost incoherent. However, the loose narrative running through the story centers on Keel's investigation and the growing threat posed by the Men in Black. In fact, the MIB play an even more prominent role in Keel's work than that of their progenitor, Barker. As one reads the *The Mothman Prophecies*, they discover Keel becoming increasingly paranoid about the Men in Black, who he claimed were terrorizing him through unsettling telephone calls to his New York residence. However, John C. Sherwood revealed in another exposé about Gray Barker for *Skeptical Inquirer* in 2002 that Barker had likely been hoaxing Keel with the phone calls and that Keel had privately written to people he trusted that he suspected as much, though he did not include them in his book.

As Aaron Gulyas, a historian of paranormal subcultures and conspiracy theories, outlines in his podcast *The Saucer Life*, Keel's suspicious nature led him to believe that there were UFO bases spread throughout the Ohio Valley and that there was some kind of "military-like buildup" afoot. Keel further thought that seemingly friendly characters like Indrid Cold were engaged in an elaborate disinformation campaign to lull people into a false sense of security about extraterrestrials and that outlandish monsters like Mothman were "creations of the UFO people" to encourage ridicule among the general public.

The book's other major theme is prophecy, and it fuels an unease in Keel that all of the paranormal activity in the Ohio Valley was leading up to something bad. He writes about a conversation with Point Pleasant resident Virginia Thomas, who said she was having disturbing dreams: "I had a terrible nightmare. There were a lot of people drowning in the river and Christmas packages were floating everywhere in the water."

It is tempting to discount the "prophetic" aspect of the book as an apocryphal flourish added by Keel years after the fact, when he knew about the bridge collapse, but his November 3, 1967 letter to Mary Hyre seems to indicate Keel and others really did have a sense of foreboding in the weeks before the disaster:

> *Mary, I have good reasons for suspecting that* [there] *may soon be a disaster in the Pt. Pleasant area which will not seem to be related to the UFO mystery. A plant along the river may either blow up or burn down. Possibly the Navy installation in Pt. Pleasant will be the center of such a disaster. A lot of people may be hurt. If this should happen, notify me as soon as you can, and write the story normally. Don't even hint to anybody anything about this.*

At the time of this writing, the authors are unaware of any claims that the Keel correspondence is illegitimate or a later hoax.

The events in Point Pleasant occurred at a pivotal time in Keel's life, during which he was developing a paranormal "theory of everything" that made use of some of Charles Fort's thinking from half a century earlier. He began to expound on some of these unorthodox ideas in his 1970 book *Operation Trojan Horse*, in which he mentions Mothman briefly. Keel had come to reject the "extraterrestrial thesis" that UFOs were physical spacecraft piloted by flesh-and-blood visitors from another planet in the material universe. In the book *Operation Trojan Horse*, Keel cites example after example from folklore and mythology where people said they encountered angels, demons, ghosts, monsters, UFOs, aliens, gods, poltergeists, fairies and, yes, even Mothmen and concludes that these similar encounters are all manifestations of the same phenomena. What people are actually seeing when they witness anything supernatural, he writes, are "ultraterrestrials."

In this "Keelian" worldview, which he further fleshed out in later writings, there exists a higher dimensional reality of which our physical universe is only one inferior part. That extradimensional realm intersects with our world in places he called "window areas," where ultraterrestrials can manifest in a multitude of ways. Keel suspected each state likely had several of these window areas that opened and closed periodically, and there just happened to be one parked over the Ohio Valley from 1966 to 1967. Mothman, Indrid Cold, the UFOs, the MIB—all of it was due to ultraterrestrials. The only mystery that remained for Keel was why such beings would bother to invade our reality.

While Keel's beliefs fall well outside the mainstream (to say the least), his influential writings and theories are considered classics in modern occultism. His view that UFOs are extradimensional in origin and not from another planet lives on in a significant portion of the modern UFO community that enjoys debating with the more traditional nuts-and-bolts UFOs-are-alien-ships camp. Echoes of his ideas, though often repackaged, can be found across paranormal subcultures from Bigfoot enthusiasts who think Sasquatch travels to and from our world via portals and ghost hunters who think reputedly haunted sites represent thin areas in the fabric between realms to new-age adherents of a trickster who teasingly manifests all supernatural phenomena for its own amusement.

Despite being an enduring favorite among paranormal enthusiasts, Mothman fell out of the national consciousness in the 1980s. The legend did get a nod in the fifth season of *The X-Files*, in which FBI agents Fox Mulder and Dana Scully investigate camouflaged humanoids with red eyes in the backwoods of Florida. Mulder even makes a somewhat butchered reference to Mothman and Point Pleasant.

The legend started to regain popularity in the late 1990s and early 2000s. A Point Pleasant business owner named Jeff Wamsley began selling Mothman T-shirts through his record shop. He noticed strong interest in the incredible story, especially among those not from West Virginia. He and Danny Sergent Jr., a local web developer, launched MothmanLives.com in 2000, making the Mothman legend accessible to a global audience. Two years later, the pair published *Mothman: The Facts Behind the Legend*, a collection of newspaper clippings, interviews, written eyewitness accounts and correspondence between Keel and his Point Pleasant contacts.

Many moviegoers around the world were introduced to Mothman for the first time in 2002, when Sony Pictures released *The Mothman Prophecies*, starring Richard Gere and Laura Linney. The film can be seen as director Mark Pellington's loose interpretation of Keel's book rather than a strict adaptation of the Mothman legend. For example, Gere plays a fictional *Washington Post* reporter named John Klein rather than the paranormal writer Keel. The film struggled at the box office and was largely regarded as a disappointment by critics who thought its screenplay was confusing and its cinematography chaotic.

While not a blockbuster, *The Mothman Prophecies* film served as a catalyst for renewed national interest in this strange folktale. Point Pleasant, which suffered its share of Rust Belt woes, has become the gold standard for how a site can leverage its paranormal reputation for economic revitalization.

In the fall after the film's release, Wamsley put on the first ever Mothman Festival as a celebration of his town's unusual heritage. The first Mothman Festival was a small, community-based affair, but the event has grown consistently year over year to become a pilgrimage site for paranormal enthusiasts. Today, well over ten thousand attendees descend on Point Pleasant each September. The festival features numerous vendors, music performances, a lecture series from paranormal investigators, bus tours of the TNT Area, cosplay contests and even a 5K run.

Growing demand in Point Pleasant for Mothman tourism prompted Wamsley to close his struggling music shop and open "The World's Only Mothman Museum" in 2005. The Mothman Museum displays several archival documents related to the first 1966 sightings, newspaper clippings, props from the movie and some of John Keel and Mary Hyre's belongings. The museum store sells everything from Mothman-themed coffee mugs to stuffed animals.

The Mothman Museum in Point Pleasant, West Virginia. *Kevin Moore.*

The Mothman Prophecies movie led Main Street Point Pleasant, the downtown revitalization committee, to commission a public statue of Mothman to be placed in the heart of downtown. They approached a retired welder named Bob Roach, who was known for his stainless steel art. What Roach unveiled in 2003, with special guest John Keel in attendance, was a thirteen-foot-tall, gleaming, red-eyed monster. Getting a picture with Mothman has since become a bucket list item for thousands. "I don't care how cold it is, there's people here every day," a committee member told the website Roadside America.

Beyond West Virginia, Mothman is a staple in national paranormal media. It has been the subject of several cryptozoological documentaries and countless paranormal investigation television shows, such as the History Channel's *The UnXplained* and *MonsterQuest* and Discovery's *Expedition X*,

Left: A mannequin of Mothman in the Mothman Museum. *Kevin Moore*.

Opposite: *Mothman Statue*, metal sculpture, Bob Roach, 2003. *Kevin Moore*.

which have all embarked on fruitless quests into the TNT Area in the hopes of catching Mothman on camera.

Mothman has made cameos in a handful of videogames over the years. Most notably, the creature appears in the postapocalyptic world depicted in *Fallout 76* (2018). In the game, a prequel in the *Fallout* series, the player emerges from a fallout shelter in rural West Virginia decades after a future nuclear exchange between the United States and China. As players explore the barren wasteland that features several overgrown landmarks from present-day West Virginia, they begin to be stalked by several varieties of mutated Mothmen and learn that the cryptid has become the focus of worship for a cult of fallout survivors.

Even the Men in Black, who feature so prominently in the works of Barker and Keel, have entered the modern cultural zeitgeist. Numerous books have been written by paranormal investigators about allegedly real encounters with the MIB, and they have remained an evergreen topic of speculation among broadcasts like *Coast to Coast AM*. Much of Barker's mythos inspired author Lowell Cunningham and illustrator Sandy Carruthers to create *The*

Men in Black comic book in 1990. The comic was turned into the highly successful science-fiction comedy film *Men in Black* (1997), starring Will Smith and Tommy Lee Jones, which went on to inspire two sequels and a spinoff.

Besides inspiring media and tourism, Mothman lives on in American folklore; people still claim to see Mothman. Beginning in 2011, paranormal investigators in Chicago began getting calls from people saying something reminiscent of Mothman was appearing across the city. The alleged "flap" hit a fever pitch in 2017, with twenty-one sightings being reported in the first half of the year alone, according to one paranormal researcher interviewed by the *Chicago Tribune*. The *Tribune* reporter likely summed up most Chicagoans' attitudes: "I remain skeptical…but I find the accounts entertaining."

What once belonged to southeastern Ohio and northwestern West Virginia now enjoys a global stage. Mothman-esque creatures have allegedly played witness to history's most infamous disasters: New York City on September 11, 2001, the Chernobyl Nuclear Power Plant in Pripyat, Ukraine, in 1986 and Fukushima Prefecture in Japan in 2011, prior to the triple disaster that saw an earthquake, tsunami and partial nuclear meltdown devastate the region. However, the legitimacy of some of these reported sightings has been questioned, and most appear to have been reported months or years after the fact.

These international stories indicate that Mothman has become what folklorist Eleanor Ann Hasken calls a "creature of omen." Hasken elegantly argues in her 2022 doctoral dissertation, "The Migration of a Local Legend: The Case of Mothman," that Keel's emphasis on Mothman as a visiting harbinger of doom in the thirteen months leading up the Silver Bridge Collapse established Mothman as a transitory myth instead of Point Pleasant's hometown cryptid.

"The 'creature of omen' component…aids in the migration process by ultimately weakening the place-based connection that ties the narrative to Point Pleasant," she writes. "As the creature becomes primarily associated with narratives of disaster prediction rather than with the place of Point Pleasant, the legend is no longer contingent on the inclusion of Point Pleasant to be understood and reproduced." It is likely the legend of Mothman will continue to be invoked in the wake of disasters as Mothman's popularity grows.

As we have seen, Mothman has matured and flown away from its Ohio Valley nest. It's doubtful Mothman will ever supplant Bigfoot's pride of place in the national psyche, but there is something about the complexity, strangeness and backwoods folksiness of this legend that mesmerizes audiences in a way that more traditional monster and ghost legends can't quite match. Perhaps this is why the infamous Men in Black are said to have worked so fervently to keep word of Mothman from getting out.

PART II

GHOSTLY TALES

7

THE ELMORE RIDER

Elmore is a small town of nearly 1,500 residents nestled beside the Portage River in Ottawa County in northwestern Ohio. Founded in 1851, the town was once home to the Elmore Manufacturing Company, a business ancestor of both General Motors and Whirlpool Corporation, as well as a beryllium plant that contributed to the U.S. space program. While some of the industry may have left Elmore, a century-old legend remains.

While the essence of this oft-repeated story has remained mostly unchanged, residents in and around Elmore have developed different names for it: Spook Light, the Elmore Rider or the Headless Motorcyclist. Even the authors, who were both raised in Northwest Ohio, grew up calling the legend different names. For the sake of consistency, we will use the name "Elmore Rider" in this book, which seems to be the most commonly used name in paranormal literature nationwide.

According to folklore, a soldier returning from Europe after World War I rode his motorcycle to his girlfriend's house, only to discover that she had married another man during his absence. The veteran, feeling betrayed, sped away in a rage. He took a turn too quickly and crashed his motorbike into the railing of a bridge, severing his head from his body.

The core of the legend claims that the rider continues to reenact his fateful ride and can be observed crashing into the bridge each year on the anniversary of his death, March 21. In order to summon the apparition, spectators must perform a ritual of parking their car near the bridge on the night of the anniversary and then blinking their headlights and honking their horn.

Like all urban legends, the story of the Elmore Rider is somewhat blurred at the edges. For example, the version of this story that appears in the 1991 book *Haunted Ohio* by Chris Woodyard holds that the rider stormed into the house to confront his girlfriend and her new husband. As told by the popular paranormal website and podcast *Astonishing Legends*, the rider snuck into his love's home to surprise her, only to have her scream in his face at the sight him still alive. In *Ghost Hunting Ohio: On the Road Again*, paranormal writer John Kachuba says the rider crashed into a ravine, not a bridge. Still other iterations hold that the rider crashed into a barbed wire fence near the bridge rather than into the bridge itself. This version is perhaps more conducive to the decapitation narrative. Other tellings blame inclement weather and not road rage for the soldier's death.

The idea that most myths contain at least some kernel of truth is a common axiom, but in the case of the Elmore Rider, that kernel has eluded researchers for decades. No one has been able to find any documentary evidence that a decapitating motorcycle accident near Elmore ever occurred. Even the site of the accident remains a subject of debate, since it is unclear which bridge in the area could be the culprit. The legend says the accident took place along a narrow, two-lane road that runs north–south, but confusing the matter is the fact that this five-mile road has two names (Slemmer-Portage Road for the northern section and Fought Road for the southern section) and crosses five creeks in the vicinity of Elmore. The leading candidate, according to most recent sources, is the southernmost option, Muddy Creek Bridge along Fought Road.

If the story of the Elmore Rider can't be associated with a documented motorcycle accident or even pinpointed to a specific place, where does this tale come from? Like most urban legends, no one can point to a single first telling. However, we can attempt to determine how long people have been talking about a ghostly rider and trace how the story has changed over time.

The legend of the Elmore Rider goes back at least to the 1960s, according to newspaper records. On Halloween 1986, the *Port Clinton News Herald* ran a summary of what was then already a popular legend. Interestingly, the *News Herald* identified a site on Slemmer-Portage Road, about four miles north of Muddy Creek Bridge, as the commonly accepted spot at the time. One of the article's interviewees, Nancy Almroth, a woman in her thirties, recalled first hearing the legend when she was a teenager in the mid-1960s. Almroth also described an incident that occurred in the 1960s, when a radio station from Toledo aired a live broadcast from the suspected spot on March 21 in an attempt to summon the rider. Apparently, he was a no-show.

Nearly a decade earlier, in 1978, the *Fremont News Messenger* also ran a Halloween article on the Elmore Rider. The *News Messenger* shared three drastically different tellings of the legend that were in circulation at the time. The first, which the paper reported as the most common, involved an overly protective father who showed his disapproval of his daughter's boyfriend's new motorcycle by stringing a wire across Fought Road before one of their dates. The second claimed the whole thing was a hoax perpetrated by a farmer who was tired of his road being used as a lovers' lane by teenagers. Lastly, the *News Messenger* conveyed what is now the dominant version of the legend set just after the First World War but with directions to a bridge on Fought Road at Ninemile Creek.

Perhaps one reason the Elmore Rider legend endures is that baked into it is an invitation for the curious to come see for themselves. In its 1986 article, the *News Herald* interviewed several residents along the road who expressed their annoyance that the legend was attracting so many ghost hunters and thrill seekers. "Passersby from as far away as Cleveland have heard the legend and have come to find if there's any truth to it," the paper reported.

Current Ninemile Creek Bridge (constructed in 1966) on Fought Road, a second candidate for the alleged bridge. *Kevin Moore.*

One such investigation has since become so embedded with the legend itself that it is nearly impossible to find a recent source telling the tale of the Elmore Rider without also sharing the story of Richard Gill. In 1968, Gill was an English major studying folklore at nearby Bowling Green State University when he decided to perform a paranormal investigation on the anniversary of the supposed accident.

Gill and an anonymous friend went to one of the bridges armed with a camera, video camera, infrared camera and some audio equipment and positioned their car to perform the ritual. Gill told the *BGNews*, a college newspaper, in a 1987 interview, "A light appeared at the farmhouse, moved down the driveway, down the road, and disappeared in the middle of the bridge."

Gill and his friend next tried to assess the physicality of the apparition by tying string across the bridge and summoning the light again. According to Gill, the light repeated the motion, passing through the string without breaking it. The pair next tried to examine the phenomena more closely, with the friend standing in the middle of the bridge while Gill performed the ritual a third time. As Gill told the *BGNews*, "His right arm was ripped up and he had cuts and bruises all over his face. He had no recollection of what had happened to him. By now I was really scared. I was ready to leave."

Despite being assaulted by the rider, Gill and his friend devised yet another experiment. This time, they summoned the light and "gunned" their car so that the phenomenon would chase them. "I had to slow down to make the turn," he said. "And as I did the light caught up to us. It passed through us as we got to the edge of the bridge." At this point, the pair had had enough ghostly encounters for one night and drove home.

Around 2015, Gill recounted the entire investigation in a video interview with his son. While he never specifically says which bridge he visited, based on his description, his encounter most likely occurred at the Wolf Creek Bridge, the northernmost bridge on Slemmer-Portage Road. He said that while most of their equipment recorded nothing, on each attempt, they were able to pick up a high-pitched hum on a microphone that is sensitive to frequencies beyond human hearing and a bright light on an infrared camera, which would indicate there was a source of heat.

Years later, after Gill returned from service in Vietnam, he published an account of his investigation in the *Journal of the Ohio Folklore Society* in 1972. He worked as an English teacher at the time but continued his hobby of investigating the paranormal. Dubbed a real-life "ghostbuster" by the *BGNews*, Gill investigated supposed hauntings in people's homes as a free service and was more often than not able to provide concerned families with natural

The current Wolf Creek Bridge (constructed in 2004) on Slemmer-Portage Road, likely the site visited by Richard Gill. *Kevin Moore.*

explanations for their observed activity. He told the paper that he returned to the bridge in Elmore several times over the years in an effort to re-create his 1968 experience, but he never saw the light again. Unfortunately, Gill passed away in 2018 and could not be interviewed for this book.

Later generations of paranormal investigators have also attempted to re-create Gill's now legendary investigation. Fringe Paranormal, a ghost hunting group from Toledo, told the *Port Clinton News Herald* in 2014 that they had attempted five or six investigations of the Muddy Creek Bridge, which they contend is *the* bridge, but to no avail. Another group in the area, Haunted Toledo, has attempted investigations on several of the supposed bridges but have yet to see the rider materialize, according to their vlog.

Richard Gill's supposed encounter with the Elmore Rider has become synonymous with the legend and serves the role of giving a somewhat common folklore tale a feeling of modern credibility and helps attach it to Ottawa County. However, belief in a headless motorcyclist is not unique to Elmore. A nearly identical urban legend is told among residents of Oxford in southwestern Ohio. In the Ghost Biker or Oxford Light legend, a young

The current Muddy Creek Bridge (constructed in 2009) on Fought Road, a site preferred by local paranormal investigation groups. *Kevin Moore*.

A supposed dead man's curve, where Oxford-Milford Road meets Earhart Road near Oxford, Ohio. *Kevin Moore*.

man, this time a World War II veteran, was riding his motorcycle to meet his girlfriend when he approached a sharp bend where Earhart Road meets Oxford-Milford Road (or possibly the curve on Buckley Road) when he slid off the berm, only to be decapitated by a barbed-wire fence. To this day, Miami University students summon the motorcycle's spectral light by traveling to various roads around Oxford and flashing their lights three times.

Looking farther afield than just the Buckeye State, one will find headless motorcyclists haunting roadways across the country. Even the Canadian town of Port Perry in Ontario tells the story of a poor motorcyclist who lost his battle with a barbed-wire fence.

The tale is familiar enough to serve as a trope in popular entertainment. In 1975, a television series, *Kolchak: The Night Stalker*, featured an episode about a headless biker who wielded a sword while on the ghostly hunt for the biker gang responsible for his murder. The series, which starred Darren McGavin as a news reporter who investigated the paranormal, was canceled after only one season but became a cult classic in syndication. It was influential enough that Chris Carter later credited *Kolchak* as one of his inspirations in creating *The X-Files*.

The rider also appeared in an episode of *The Real Ghostbusters*, the animated children's spinoff of the classic Ivan Reitman movie, titled "The Headless Motorcyclist." In the cartoon, which aired in 1987, the Headless Motorcyclist is revealed to be a modern manifestation of Washington Irving's Headless Horseman, who has been haunting Ichabod Crane's descendants for generations. Of course, that is until Crane's most recent descendant, Kate, calls the Ghostbusters for help. It is worth wondering to what extent these depictions in mass media contributed to the headless motorcyclist legend being exported to new locations.

The Headless Motorcyclist as a concept is so widespread that one can think of the character less as a singular tale and more as a modern expression of an old genre of folklore. In *The Real Ghostbusters* cartoon, the show's writers made the Headless Motorcyclist and the Headless Horseman from "The Legend of Sleepy Hollow" explicitly the same entity. From a folkloric perspective, that may not have been far off.

In Washington Irving's short story (as well as its countless adaptations), the Headless Horseman is the vengeful spirit of a Hessian soldier who was decapitated by a cannonball during the American Revolution. The Elmore Rider, although angry from having his love spurned, is a veteran of World War I. In the open-ended conclusion of Irving's short story, we see a terrified Ichabod Crane being run down across a bridge by the Headless Horseman, a scene not unlike what is said to happen to those bold enough to summon the rider on March 21.

Myths of headless riders haunting roadways have a long history in western folklore all the way back to Celtic cultures. Writing for the *Irish Times*, Jessica Traynor, the director of the EPIC Irish Emigration Museum, describes how Irish ghost tales followed Irish migration through western Europe and eventually found new homes in North America. One particular myth that has endured in countless folklore traditions involves an entity called the Dullahan, or "dark man." This spirit is a manifestation of the Celtic deity Crom Dubh, who was worshiped through sacrifices involving decapitation. When Christianity arrived in Ireland and displaced the worship of local indigenous gods, tradition held that the spiteful Crom Dubh became a headless rider, often pulling a black coach, from which he called travelers to early deaths along Europe's roadways.

Thomas J. Westropp, a twentieth-century Irish folklorist, published a series of articles on the many folk stories told by the residents of County Clare in Ireland in the journal *Folk-Lore: Transactions of the Folk-Lore Society* in 1910. Westropp began his study on the Dullahan by trying to situate "headless coach" tales within the broader history Irish folklore. "The 'headless coach' or 'coach a bower' seems of far later date than the banshee," he wrote. "Ghostly chariots such as that of Cuchulain [a demigod in Irish mythology] figure in very early tales, but neither their appearance nor their sound foretold death. In Clare, at sight or sound of the coach, all gates should be thrown open, and then it will not stop at the house to call for a member of the family, but only foretell the death of some relative at a distance."

Westropp recounted one contemporary urban legend that was still being told by locals in County Clare when he conducted his survey in the early 1900s:

On the night of December 11th, 1876, a servant of the MacNamaras was going his rounds at Ennistymon, a beautiful spot in a wooded glen, with a broad stream falling in a series of cascades. In the dark he heard the rumbling of wheels on the back avenue, and, knowing from the hour and place that no "mortal vehicle" could be coming, concluded that it was the death coach and ran on, opening the gates before it. He had just time to open the third gate and throw himself on his face beside it, at the bank, before he "heard a coach go clanking past." It did not stop at the house, but passed on, and the sound died away. On the following day Admiral Sir Burton MacNamara died in London.

Readers of "The Legend of Sleepy Hollow" will notice similarities to folktales of the Dullahan, especially the element of a frightening chase along a deserted nighttime road by an otherworldly rider. Some of these same characteristics seem to persist in the stories from the country roads near Elmore.

Today, Elmore embraces its famous headless motorcyclist. The Harris-Elmore Public Library has developed a ghost walk tour that takes visitors to fifteen supposedly haunted sites in town. While the bridges on Slemmer-Portage Road are too far to walk to, tour guides still discuss the legend of the Elmore Rider. According to some tellings of the legend, the bridges near Elmore now attract so many thrill seekers every March that the local police spend the night shooing them away, although Elmore Chief of Police Jeffrey Harrison knows "of no significant issues the local police officers have encountered in the past 20 years in relation to the event other than an occasional lost motorist."

The town has also become well known for a unique Halloween tradition inspired by the rider theme, the Count Krumnow Tombstone Derby. Named for the founder of the Elmore Historical Society, "Count" Lowell Krumnow, who was enthusiastic for Halloween, the first Tombstone Derby was held in 2005 and featured a hodgepodge parade of tractors, go-karts and lawnmowers decorated as coffins, hearses and, yes, black coaches. The citizens of Elmore and the surrounding area continue to dress up in their Halloween best and show off their haunted vehicles while they enjoy a family-friendly Halloween festival.

Just as Westropp observed an evolution in the archetype of the Headless Coachman in Irish folklore a century ago, we have seen how this tale has adapted to American culture since coming to the United States. The headless coach may have "gone the way of the horse and buggy," but this timeless tale lives on by riding a Harley.

8

GORE ORPHANAGE

The story of Gore Orphanage has all the hallmarks of a classic ghost tale that is told around the campfire or while exploring the woods after dark, looking for a good scare.

It goes something like this: in the late 1800s, a family or person named Gore ran an orphanage in a rural area just outside Vermilion, today a picturesque small town about forty-two miles west of Cleveland on the Lake Erie shore.

The Gores treated the children horribly, forcing them to wear rags, providing them with barely enough food to survive and beating them for the slightest perceived wrongdoing. One night, the orphanage caught fire and burned to the ground, killing the miserable youngsters.

In another version of the tale, the Gores were kind people who loved and cared for the orphans as if they were their own children. This version blames the blaze on a crazed local or drifter who wanted to cause mayhem.

Still other versions claim one of the children accidentally knocked over a lantern, igniting the fire.

Regardless of the details, the gist of the legend is that the children died a grisly, horrifying death and are not enjoying a peaceful eternal rest. Those who go to the woods where the orphanage was at night hear their tortured screams for help and sometimes see their ghostly bodies wandering the woods. Others see flashes of light and return to their cars to find them dotted with tiny handprints.

Gore Orphanage Road outside Vermilion is home to one of Ohio's most famous urban legends. *Kristina Smith.*

For decades, this story has persisted and has been featured in books, publications and other media. Teens have videoed themselves walking through the woods at night, jumping at any sound they hear.

Even the bridge over the Vermilion River on Gore Orphanage Road leading to the area that is believed to be haunted is covered with graffiti, including the ominous warning: "Do not enter."

But almost none of the Gore Orphanage story is true.

It is, however, a great example of how urban legends form and persist through generations. The story meshes several kernels of truth from events that occurred in Ohio and Indiana to create one of Ohio's most popular ghost stories.

There was no Gore Orphanage. The orphanage that was in the area was south of Vermilion near the village of Birmingham and opened there in 1903. It did not burn down, but there were accounts of its residents being whipped and forced to eat meager food that was sometimes cooked in the same pot that was used to clean the dirty laundry.

The true story of the orphanage, which was actually called the Light and Hope Orphanage (also sometimes known as the Light of Hope Orphanage), and its founders is far more interesting.

ORPHANAGE IN INDIANA

The story begins in Berne, Indiana, a small town south of Fort Wayne that was established by Swiss immigrants and named for Bern, Switzerland. There, John Abraham Sprunger and his wife, Katharina "Katie" Sprunger, began a missionary society that helped people throughout the world.

Katharina Sprunger and Reverend John A. Sprunger moved the Light and Hope Orphanage in 1903 to the village of Birmingham near Vermilion, Ohio, from Berne, Indiana. *Photograph courtesy of Max Haines.*

John Sprunger was a young boy when his family moved from Switzerland to the United States and settled the Berne area with other Mennonite families. He grew to be a hardworking young man and a pillar of the community.

He was twenty-seven years old when he married Katie, who was his first cousin. He owned a sawmill and dry goods and grocery store, and the couple was very active in their church.

"Berne owes a great deal to John A. Sprunger," his obituary in the *Berne Witness* read on October 3, 1911. "In its early days, he was the soul and life of it. He had a keen business instinct, was farsighted and clear sighted and made a success of nearly everything he undertook to do."

In 1888, a fire destroyed the mill and the store, causing $25,000 in damage, according to *Light and Hope: The Story of the Rev. John A. Sprunger and Katharina Sprunger and Their Heritage*, by Max Haines. John Sprunger rebuilt, and the businesses thrived.

Fire would be something that would plague the Sprungers' ventures throughout their lives. Tragedy seemed to follow them. Each of their four children died in their early years.

After the death of their six-year-old daughter, Hillegonda, the devastated John Sprunger fell ill. He decided to become a minister, and his health improved.

In 1889, the Sprungers traveled to Switzerland and stayed there for about a year and a half, according to Haines's book. The trip was a religious retreat of sorts, and it was in Switzerland that they felt called to start an orphanage and create a network of deaconesses, young women who worked as missionaries.

When they returned, John Sprunger turned control of his businesses over to his partners and focused on the church and missionary work.

The Sprungers opened the Light and Hope Orphanage in 1893 in Berne, Indiana. The children there were orphans or "half orphans," children of divorced couples or who had only one surviving parent who no longer wanted them, according to *Light and Hope*.

The Sprungers also opened deaconess hospitals and homes in Chicago and Cleveland. In Chicago, the missionary women went to the worst parts of the city and brought young women who were prostitutes to live there and improve their circumstances, according to Haines's book. The Chicago facility also took in unmarried pregnant women and helped them find places to live after they gave birth.

Throughout the decades, the Sprungers sent missionaries throughout the world and built more deaconess hospitals. John Sprunger started his own Light and Hope Publishing Company and circulated a monthly newsletter detailing the work of these different ventures.

FIRES AT SPRUNGER MISSIONS IN BERNE AND CLEVELAND

In the early hours of April 19, 1895, the girls' dormitory at the Light and Hope Orphanage in Berne caught fire. A deaconess found the blaze in the kitchen ceiling around 4:00 a.m. The cause wasn't determined, according to Haines's book.

Forty girls, ages one through sixteen, and four deaconesses lived in the dorm. Most got out by jumping out of windows or climbing down the fire escape, but three girls died.

The Sprungers, who were awakened by someone pounding on their door shortly after the blaze was discovered, rushed to the scene.

"They could hear the girls screaming even before they went out of the house," Haines wrote in *Light and Hope*. "They and many others in town would remember the screams for many years."

The Sprungers rebuilt the girls' dorm later that year. In August, another fire broke out, this time in the boys' dorm.

At bedtime, a curtain blew into a burning gas jet. Fortunately, a passerby saw the flames, ran into the dorm and was able to extinguish the fire before it got out of control, according to Haines's book.

"The children of the home were all put out in their night dresses, terrorized, crying and terribly frightened by the memory of the former fire that occurred there only a few months ago," the *Berne Witness* reported on August 31, 1899, as quoted in Haines's book. "This fire and the expense it incurred upon the town is nothing but the result of careless neglect, to which was also due the death of the three children last April. And all grows out of the incompetency of the managers of the home."

Perhaps these fires at the orphanage in Berne helped fuel the Vermilion Gore Orphanage story.

Or maybe the story of an earlier fire at the Sprungers' deaconess hospital in Cleveland morphed into part of the legend. The Cleveland hospital burned in 1894, killing some of the patients and one of the deaconesses. It was rebuilt in 1899 and remained open until 1934, according to Haines's book.

In addition to fires, bad publicity tended to follow the Sprungers. John Sprunger and the editor of the *Berne Witness*, the local newspaper in Berne, did not get along, Haines said in an interview.

The editor, Fred Rohrer, had been Sprunger's assistant at the church, and they often had opposing views. Rohrer later left Light and Hope and began publishing the *Witness*, which usually reported negatively on the Sprungers' work.

Rohrer wrote editorials and added comments to articles, sharing his opinions about the Sprungers' treatment of the children and what he considered the ineptitude of those running the orphanage. John Sprunger wrote a detailed response that was published in the newspaper outlining what he considered the errors in the articles and the truth of what went on at the orphanage.

"Our home is open any time for inspection," John Sprunger wrote in his rebuttal printed in the *Berne Witness* on June 27, 1901. "Any officers who know anything about institutions are welcome. We will be glad to have them compare it with any others in the state."

ORPHANAGE MOVES TO OHIO

In 1902, the Light and Hope Publishing Company moved to Cleveland, and the Sprungers bought a farm near the village of Birmingham, Ohio, to relocate the Light and Hope Orphanage. Birmingham is about forty miles west of Cleveland.

"At that same time, the need was felt keenly at the orphanage for a country home where we could buy sufficient land to raise the main part of our crops," Sprunger wrote in his April 1909 newsletter, as quoted by Haines's book. "By searching around a place was found near the Vermilion River, Lorain County, Ohio."

Sprunger bought several buildings and farms in the area and put them together as a 543-acre complex that housed 100 to 120 children in boys' and girls' dormitories, farm buildings and schools. The orphanage opened in Ohio in November 1903. There, the children called John Sprunger "Pa Sprunger" and Katie Sprunger "Ma Sprunger," according to Haines's book.

The boys were sent out to area farms to work during the day, said Rich Tarrant, a curator of the Vermilion History Museum. In 1906, a nursery for infants was added, according to an article in the *Vermilion News* on July 6, 1916.

This undated photograph of the orphanage was taken when it was located in Ohio. Katharina Sprunger can be seen in the center of the photograph, wearing a long, white apron. *Missionary Church Archives and Historical Collections.*

"The children are educated about the same as in the average school in the country," Sprunger wrote in his newsletter. "They attend the school from the age of six to fifteen years. And those that are more gifted and desire more education are sent to school outside the home school. Children are received as before mentioned, regardless of any church creed or denomination, and probably half of them come from such parents as do not attend any church."

ALLEGATIONS OF MISTREATMENT, NEGLECT

Despite the orphanage moving to Ohio, negative media coverage continued. It was not uncommon for some of the children to run away, and some shared stories with the local newspaper of being mistreated and being given meager and outright disgusting food.

In 1908, orphan Bennie Sutliff, who was fourteen or fifteen at the time, ran away from the orphanage after living there for seven years and moved in with a local family, the *Vermilion News* reported on January 21, 1909. A judge in Elyria, the county seat of Lorain County, determined the boy could stay with the family.

In September that year, the newspaper reported that more boys and girls had run away from the orphanage and that locals had taken them in. All "reported misusage."

W.B. Glatz brought a court case against the orphanage, apparently on behalf of his three grandchildren who were housed there, according to the *Vermilion News*. On Friday, September 10, 1909, the newspaper reported on a hearing in that case, which lasted three days.

The hearing provided a deeper look into the residents' allegations and included testimony from Katie Sprunger that seemed to confirm some of the reports of neglect.

Former resident Tom Baker, sixteen, had run away because of "harsh treatment" and was now living with a Vermilion farmer. He said the residents were often served calves' lungs and heads for food and that despite there being cows on the farm, they received butter no more than once a week and rarely had pepper and sugar.

They weren't given enough blankets to stay warm at night in the winter, and the rooms were infested with vermin, he testified.

"On occasions, he remembered rats had crawled onto the beds and bitten the boys while they lay asleep," the newspaper reported. "When questioned regarding the bathing facilities at the home, Baker stated that there was only

The orphanage was located above Swift's Hollow near the village of Birmingham. The road that once led there is no longer in use and disappears into the woods. *Kristina Smith.*

one bathtub for the boys, which they were allowed to use once every two weeks, and that on several occasions fifteen to twenty youngsters had been compelled to use the same water."

Another former resident, George Lambert, eighteen, confirmed Baker's allegations and also said John Sprunger and the farm overseers beat him and others until "great raw welts appeared on their bodies inflicted by the use of the strap," the newspaper reported.

Lambert said he ultimately ran away because he "wanted to learn" and that the boys were only allowed to attend school when there was no work to do on the grounds.

Defense witnesses gave a completely different story, although the newspaper did not cast most of them in a favorable light.

Charles Welty of Cleveland, a former resident of the home, gave testimony that opposed Baker's and Lambert's, the newspaper reported. It did not, however, specify what he said but described him as "a rather privileged character, as he was appointed as an overseer, during the latter part of his stay at the orphanage."

Peter Fiebach of Henrietta Township said he thought the home was run in a correct manner and that he thought several of the boys were "incorrigible."

"On one occasion, two of them tipped over his sap buckets for which they were thrashed by Mr. Sprunger, but not enough to suit him, he added," according to the newspaper.

At this point, Humane Officer Lawrence, whose full name was not mentioned in the article, asked Fiebach about his reputation among the neighbors.

"Fiebach was compelled to admit that he was not overly popular," the newspaper reported.

The paper also quoted John A. Muller, describing him as someone who worked on the farm "for the sake of the children," saying that "nothing more could be asked for their comfort and maintenance."

The following week, Katie Sprunger, who supervised the nearly one hundred children living at the orphanage at that time, testified.

She said butter was served nearly every morning and that the children were fed ham, bacon, tongue and hash, as well as the lungs of cattle, according to the *Vermilion News*. They also had been served heads of cattle in the past, she testified.

"Corn, which is to be dried, is first boiled in a huge kettle in the laundry, the same kettle being used to steam the white underwear worn by the children, which is boiled before being washed, she added that the kettle was cleaned first before the corn was placed in it," the newspaper reported.

Katie Sprunger testified she could not remember when the children had been served eggs because she had too much else to do.

"She admitted that four or five girls bathed in the same water, which was carried from the roof of the building into a tank in the bathroom," the newspaper reported.

Additionally, the newspaper made allegations that a girl suffering from an eye disease was given salve and told to rely on prayers to heal her. The newspaper did not identify the girl or attribute the allegation to any testimony.

"There seems to be something radically wrong with the management of the institution," the newspaper opined. "Although we have given only a small part of the testimony, it brings to light a condition of things, which could be improved especially in regard to cleanliness and comfort."

On September 16, 1909, the *Vermilion News* reported that the investigation into the orphanage was completed. The state of Ohio had no laws governing orphanages, so no further action could be taken.

"It seems that some of the accusations were admitted while others were not verified," the newspaper reported. "The humane officer says he will watch affairs at the house."

Another result of the hearing was that the judge allowed W.B. Glatz to take custody of his grandchildren and adopt them, the newspaper reported.

By the time of the hearings, John Sprunger was in poor health. He had suffered a stroke in 1907 that left him partially paralyzed.

Keeping up the orphanage and farm had become too financially difficult for the Sprungers, according to *Light and Hope*. In July 1911, John Sprunger transferred ownership of the orphanage to the Cleveland Bible Institute, which continued to operate it.

Two months later, he died of another stroke. He was fifty-nine years old.

Katie Sprunger worked for five more years until the orphanage, which was in debt, was again sold and closed.

"Financially, the project is said to never have been a success....For some time, it had been known that this home must be disbanded," the *Vermilion News* reported on July 6, 1916. "The dependents have gradually been disposed of, many being returned to relatives or guardians, some to other institutions, and a few, who seemed to have no place, were taken by Mrs. Sprunger to her old home at Berne, Indiana."

The farm was sold to Jesse M. Elliott and two associates from Columbus, according to the article. They purchased the property as an investment and planned to divide it up into smaller farms and sell them.

Katie Sprunger died of cancer of the esophagus in 1934, according to Haines's book.

Tarrant doubts that the Sprungers knowingly mistreated the children. More likely, with John Sprunger's declining health, the orphanage became too much for the couple to manage, he said.

"I think it was a pie-in-the-sky on the Sprungers' part coming from Indiana to do this orphanage," Tarrant said. "I think the perfect idea was to bring the kids, put them in a farm setting, have them work on the farm and have them be self-supporting. That was the idea, but that's not how it worked out."

Despite some of the horror stories, many of the kids found homes in the area and grew up to have happy lives, Tarrant said.

Haines interviewed William Schultz, a resident of the orphanage from 1907 to 1913, in 1992, five years before Schultz died at the age of 101. Schultz was emphatic the Sprungers were good people who were concerned with the spiritual welfare of the children, according to the account of the interview Haines shared in his book.

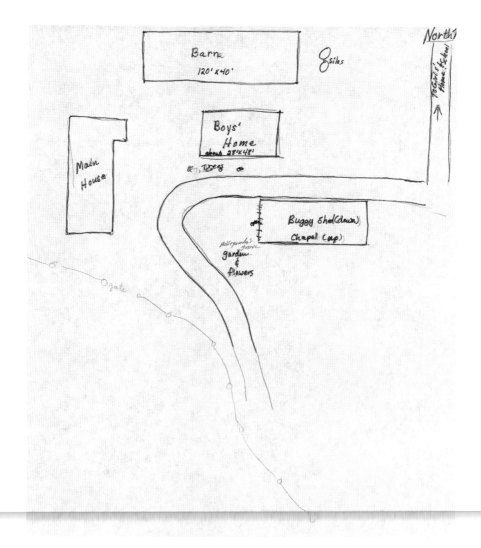

Harold Bauman, who grew up on a farm near the Light and Hope Orphanage near Birmingham, Ohio, drew this map of part of the complex. *Missionary Church Archives and Historical Collections.*

The boys worked in the fields, cut firewood and went swimming in the Vermilion River. At Christmastime, there was a tree with lit candles, and each child received a bag of candy.

"Anyone that says Ma and Pa Sprunger were bad people is a liar," Schultz told Haines. "You can tell them Bill Schultz said it, and he knew them personally."

How Did Light and Hope Turn into Gore Orphanage in Popular Lore?

The orphanage was located on a hill near Gore Orphanage Road. *Gore* was actually a surveying term used to refer to a triangular piece of land that appeared similar to a gore or hem of a skirt, Tarrant said.

"It was Gore Road before the orphanage came along," Tarrant said. "The 'Gore' only referred to the name of the road where it was located."

Because the Light and Hope Orphanage was also there, the road's name became Gore Orphanage Road. In today's vernacular, the word *gore* evokes thoughts of bloody scenes in horror movies.

Combining the name with the various fires surrounding the Sprungers and the allegations of mistreatment at the orphanage turned the story into the yarn it is today.

Two different fires in the region also might have contributed to the legend, Tarrant said.

There was a fire in the orphanage's print shop, which was in a separate building from the children's dorms, in 1910. No one was hurt, Tarrant said.

There was also a fire at a school near Cleveland that trapped and killed several children. Although the school had no connection to the orphanage, the grisly loss of young lives there might have been thrown into the Gore Orphanage legend.

"People kind of took these ideas and put them all together," Tarrant said.

So much misinformation surrounds Light and Hope that even the location of the orphanage has been misidentified for decades, Tarrant said. Haines, a minister in Berne who belongs to the church Sprunger started, clarified the location thanks to his book and his twenty years of research into the Sprungers and their missionary work.

Many believe the orphanage was located in Swift's Hollow, just outside Vermilion along the Vermilion River, at the stately home called Rosedale. The house was built by Joseph Swift and then sold to the Wilbur family.

The Sprungers then bought the property that included the house, but it was abandoned at that time and later burned down, Tarrant said.

The orphanage itself was located at the top of the hill above the hollows. The Sprungers owned buildings throughout the farm area, but Rosedale never housed any of the orphans, Tarrant said.

Rosedale was so admired in the community that Vermilion's library, the Ritter Public Library, was built to look like it. Although it is historically interesting, Rosedale had little to do with the actual story of the orphanage.

The bridge on Gore Orphanage Road over the Vermilion River is covered with graffiti, including the warning "Do Not Enter." *Kristina Smith.*

The Ritter Public Library in Vermilion was built to look like the Swift mansion, which is often mistakenly reported to be an orphanage dormitory that burned down. *Kristina Smith.*

This photograph shows one of the barns that was part of the Light and Hope Orphanage in Ohio. The photograph was taken circa 1980, more than sixty years after the orphanage closed. *Missionary Church Archives and Historical Collections.*

This circa-1980 photograph shows the inside of one of the barns that was part of the Light and Hope Orphanage in Ohio. It and the other orphanage buildings are no longer standing. *Missionary Church Archives and Historical Collections.*

Today, the orphanage buildings are gone, and the land where they stood is private property. Gore Orphanage Road narrows and disappears into the woods. "No trespassing" signs mark the area.

The Gore Orphange story has persisted through generations, because many people love a good ghost tale.

"People want to be thrilled, especially the younger people," Tarrant said. "I think when you're between say 14 and 20, it's kind of fun to go out and park on the side of the road where it's dark and think about all the things that are in the darkness."

9

THE LEGEND OF HOLCOMB WOODS

Motorists driving along State Route 6, east of Bowling Green, a college town in northwestern Ohio, will pass near a stretch of supposedly haunted woods and will almost certainly have no idea they did so. Holcomb Woods is remote, isolated and off the beaten path, making it the perfect site for an urban legend.

Holcomb Road is a narrow, two-lane country road that is a mere four miles long from end to end. It serves as only an east–west connector between two slightly larger country roads. Drivers along Route 199 between Toledo and Fostoria might notice they crossed it if they happen to be on the lookout for its poorly marked, out-of-the-way road sign. In sum, travelers on Holcomb Road are never just "passing through."

While most of Holcomb Road is bordered by corn and wheat fields, there is one quarter-mile stretch that pierces a dense patch of woods. Even on sunny days, those four hundred yards inside Holcomb Woods can seem unusually dark. It is here where local legend says ghosts reside.

According to the lore told in and around Wood County, this particular section of road was the site of a tragic school bus crash. The driver veered off the road, and the bus smashed its way through the forest before colliding with a thick tree deep inside Holcomb Woods' dark interior. The impact is said to have killed the bus driver immediately and set the bus ablaze. The gruesome legend says some or all of the children on board burned to death.

What could have caused such a horrific crash? That depends on the telling. In some versions of the story, the bus accident is simply that: an

The western entrance to Holcomb Woods. *Kevin Moore*.

accident caused by inclement weather. A more popular telling involves the driver suffering a sudden fit of rage and intentionally killing himself and his passengers. One of the more dramatic versions of the story says the bus driver was seeking revenge on a local farmer on Holcomb Road who refused to allow his daughter to date the driver's son. When the driver spotted the farmer on the roadside, he drove his bus off the road to run the farmer over before it crashed into the woods.

Today, the anguished spirits of the bus driver and children are said to roam Holcomb Woods. Visitors to the site have reported seeing apparitions, hearing a ghostly crash and having their blood run cold at the sound of children screaming and crying. Some maintain that if motorists pull off in the woods and face their car west, toward State Route 199, their radio will turn to static, and they will lose cellphone reception before seeing a spectral light race down the road and careen into the woods. Readers will notice parallels between this ritual and that of the legend of the Elmore Rider.

Given its haunted reputation, Holcomb Woods is a popular site for local teenagers looking for a scare as well as paranormal investigation groups. Sometimes, the aims of these two parties come into conflict, as

Inside Holcomb Woods. *Kevin Moore.*

they did in 2016, when Fringe Paranormal of Toledo had to abandon a planned investigation when they discovered the site was overrun with teens. A subsequent investigation by the group was largely unsuccessful, save for the discovery of some "creepy" trees and concrete pillars that had been graffitied.

One of many "No Trespassing" signs lining Holcomb Road. *Kevin Moore.*

It should be noted that Holcomb Woods is private property, a message emphasized by several "No Trespassing" signs around the property. Local students and ghost hunters investigate at their own risk. One of this book's authors can personally attest to this, as one of their relatives was driven home by a sheriff's deputy after a night of ghost hunting there.

Mira Adkins Victor Belikov Makenna Weyburne Cash Allen Bishop Childers
Sydney Schroeder Garrett Hummel Carleigh Good Kasidy Rae Lynn

The Legend of Holcomb Road

A poster for the 2018 film *The Legend of Holcomb Road* (Kasidy Rae Lynn pictured). *Matt Erman.*

What history could be fueling this influential legend? Unfortunately, the lore does not provide many details about this supposed tragic school bus accident. Michael McMaster, an education coordinator with the Wood County Museum, told the student news website BG Falcon Media in 2021 that the bus accident is a complete fabrication. "There was no bus crash ever," he said. "That legend was all because at the corner of that road, before you enter the largest forest of Wood County, the guy who owned that property in the 1970s collected junk and had a random bus from the local high school sitting in there." McMaster also attributes the popularity of John Carpenter's *Halloween* in 1978 in turning what had been a secluded lovers' lane in the 1960s into the county's favorite haunted site by the 1980s.

Even though Holcomb's infamous bus crash never occurred, it should come as no surprise that such a legend should grow around this particular road. At least twelve auto accidents and a score of injuries occurred on what was then a dirt road between 1965 and 1995. Drivers regularly flipped their cars into the ditch or collided with trees. Sadly, Holcomb Woods was even the site of two separate, tragic suicides in 1975.

The mythos surrounding Holcomb Woods has provided inspiration for Northwest Ohio's robust independent arts scene. Independent author Joseph Coley from Findlay, Ohio, featured the legend in his 2013 short story "A Night on Holcomb Road." In 2018, Capture1 Studios, a local film studio in nearby Fostoria, Ohio, released a twenty-minute short horror film, *The Legend of Holcomb Road*, as well as a forty-minute documentary on the legend titled *Holcomb Woods: Stories from Beyond the Road*.

The film's director, Matt Erman, saw the tale as a powerful tool he could use to connect with local audiences. "Everybody in the area thinks it's haunted," he told the *Toledo City Paper*. "I started going there when I was a kid, in '91, '92, and knew of the legend. When I mentioned [in an online post] that we were gonna do Holcomb Road, the post went completely viral. When this post went out, it got 150 shares, the post itself had over 150,000 views."

Erman had no trouble finding enthusiasm for the project and shot *The Legend of Holcomb Road* with a cast of over forty area residents, including several aspiring actors from local high school drama clubs. When Capture1 premiered the horror short and documentary at the Maumee Indoor Theatre, over nine hundred attendees bought out both showings. *The Legend of Holcomb Road* subsequently hit the regional indie film festival circuit, where it won awards for its special effects.

The legend of Holcomb Woods provides a textbook example of how urban legends can develop a life of their own divorced from the historical record. Despite a consensus that there is no evidence to support a fatal bus crash in the area, the Holcomb Woods story continues to grow in popularity, particularly within the local culture. The legend may be fictitious, but for residents of Northwest Ohio it is *their* legend. That sense of ownership gives this particular urban legend value above and beyond any objective truth. Stories like the legend of Holcomb Woods allow those who study folklore to consider to what extent legends can be true without actually being real.

10

MARITIME LEGENDS OF OHIO

The Black Dog of Lake Erie

The schooner peacefully sailed across Lake Erie on a quiet, starry night. Just a few crew members were still awake to navigate the boat through the calm water.

Suddenly, a large black dog crawled up onto the deck, seemingly from nowhere. The creature was completely dry, despite apparently coming from the dark, cold water below the boat.

The dog looked at the dumbfounded crew and then ran across the deck and jumped off the other side of the boat. It made no splash.

The men rushed to the side of the boat, expecting to see the animal paddling below, but the dog had vanished.

The evening was as quiet as it had been just a few seconds before—as if the dog had simply been a figment of their imagination. But the men, still shaken from the unexplainable experience, were certain of what they had seen.

The ship sailed on without incident for a day or two. Then, without warning, a gale blew in, battering the boat with waves until it sank. Its wreckage washed ashore in the following days. The entire crew had perished.

This is the legend of the Black Dog of Lake Erie. It was believed to have been the death omen for at least three doomed ships in the nineteenth century on Lake Erie and Lake Ontario.

During the late 1800s, there was no greater affront to a Great Lakes sailor than to say ,"May the Black Dog cross your deck!"

"Fifty or sixty years ago, it was not healthy even to talk about the Black Dog of Lake Erie along the waterfront," according to "Schooner Days," a column in the *Toronto Star* that was published from 1931 to 1956. "The threat to bring the beast was a threat of death; deserving of death, in the simple logic of the men who drove the lake trade when canvas was king."

The legend appears to have started with the *Mary Jane*. The ship was a three-masted schooner that sank in a gale on November 19, 1881, on its way from Port Colborne, Ontario, to Erie, Pennsylvania, according to Great Lakes Maritime Collection records at the Alpena County George N. Fletcher Public Library.

The *Mary Jane* was in the Welland Canal, which connects Lake Ontario with Lake Erie, when a large, black Newfoundland dog fell overboard and struggled mightily in the canal. The cruel crewmembers did nothing to help the poor animal and stood on the deck laughing at its violent paddling. The terrified dog finally exhausted itself and succumbed to the water.

The animal's lifeless body got stuck in the locks, which made it difficult for the locks to function properly and caused the ship to be stuck there longer than normal.

As the boat sailed on to Lake Erie, its crewmembers were dumbfounded to see the very same dog climb onto the deck, race across the boat and jump off the other side. The animal vanished.

When the boat was last seen, the weather was clear and calm. Not long after that, a gale suddenly blew in, blasting the ship with snow squalls.

The ship vanished in the storm without a trace of its wreckage, according to the legend. The Black Dog had exacted its revenge on the cruel crew.

The story of the ship vanishing, however, was untrue. Wreckage, including brown marked "*Mary Jane*" washed ashore near Dunkirk, New York, on the south shore of Lake Erie, wrote the "Schooner Days" columnists, who related the legend in several columns through the years and examined the other stories of the Black Dog.

There were no other written records found, other than those in "Schooner Days," recounting the legend itself and the incident with the dog in the Welland Canal.

Notices printed in the *Cleveland Herald* after the *Mary Jane* sank in 1881 make no mention of either a spectral dog or a pet owned by the captain or crew. Another schooner, the *Dorr*, sank the same night, and there are no mentions of an animal aboard that ship.

Two other ships, the *Thomas Home* and the *CT Jenkins*, or *IG Jenkins*, depending on the account, were believed to have fallen victim to the Black Dog.

Black Dog. *Illustration by Kari Schultz.*

The stories of the *CT Jenkins* and *IG Jenkins* are similar, as they are related through the years in "Schooner Days," so it is likely these are the same ship and that there was confusion about the correct name.

In both stories, a crewman at the wheel of the ship on a late night in 1875 was drinking cornjuice, which probably was a type of corn whiskey.

"When he was at the wheel one calm moonlight night in Lake Erie he had seen a large black dog climb up over her rail from the water, walk across the moonlit deck 'as plain as day,' climb the rail on the opposite side, and vanish into the lake," according to a "Schooner Days" column published on May 22, 1937.

The captain had brought his own dog aboard the ship for the voyage, but this sailor was convinced the dog he saw was a different one. Another "Schooner Days" telling of this story said that the sailor immediately quit but kept following the ship from port to port, warning that the captain should abandon it, lest the Black Dog's warning come true. Eventually, the captain sent his actual dog after the former sailor to chase him away.

In late 1875, the *Jenkins* sailed out onto Lake Ontario and foundered. The captain and crew were never seen again. The captain's black dog, however, survived. A farmer found the dog walking with great difficulty, as if its back legs were paralyzed, along the shore west of Oswego, New York.

This ship was most likely the *IG Jenkins*, listed as the *Isaac G. Jenkins* in the Fletcher Library's records. This ship was a wooden schooner that foundered on December 2, 1875, on Lake Ontario, near Oswego. All ten crewmen were killed.

There are no records of the *CT Jenkins* in the Fletcher Library's collection or the Bowling Green State University's Historical Collections of the Great Lakes. Similarly, there are no records of the *Thomas Home* in those databases. "Schooner Days" also reported the *Thomas Home* was a victim of the Black Dog but did not specify what happened to the ship.

THE LAKE ERIE TRIANGLE

Victoria King Heinsen, her husband at the time and two small children spent a relaxing night at Kelleys Island and boarded their boat to head back to the mainland.

As they drove out on the open water, a dense fog enveloped them. Fog and storms popping up with little notice aren't unusual on Lake Erie, the shallowest and most volatile of the Great Lakes, so the family wasn't overly concerned.

It was the mid-1980s. Electronic navigational equipment commonly used today was available at the time, but Heinsen's family did not yet have it. Her husband, however, was an excellent navigator with a compass and charts and had many years of experience piloting boats.

So, she was unnerved when he came to the back of the boat with a look of fear on his face.

"I can remember him coming back and saying, 'We're going around in circles,'" Heinsen said. "His eyes were really big, and he said, 'I do not know where we are. The compass doesn't work.'"

The family went around and around for what seemed like hours, and Heinsen's husband managed to successfully navigate the boat safely out of the fog and back to the marina in Port Clinton on the mainland.

"He was really strong, and he did battle whatever it was that was out there," she said.

The incident was something the family never forgot, and Heinsen believes it was their own run-in with what some mariners believe is the Lake Erie Triangle, Ohio's version of the Bermuda Triangle.

The triangle starts from Kelleys Island and goes 12.6 miles northwest to the Hen Islands, southwest to West Sister Island and east for 16.8 miles back to Kelleys Island, Heinsen relates in her book *Ghosts and Legends of Lake Erie's North Coast*. The triangle measures about 106 square miles.

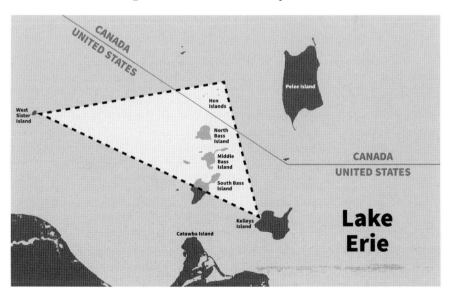

The Lake Erie Triangle stretches from Kelleys Island to the Hen Islands and West Sister Island and back to Kelleys. *Illustration by Mark Levans.*

Heinsen and boaters who have shared their experiences with her know the volatility of Lake Erie, which has an average depth of sixty-two feet and is much shallower in the islands region, with an average depth there of twenty-four feet. A calm afternoon on the water can, with little warning, quickly turn dark and violent with six- to eight-foot waves. Perhaps that is why Lake Erie is believed to be the graveyard of the most shipwrecks on the Great Lakes.

There are more than 1,700 known shipwrecks that have occurred on the lake, and only 277 of those wreckages had been discovered as of 2019, according to Ohio Sea Grant, a program of Ohio State University that has developed an online map of identified wrecks.

There are logical explanations for some of these incidents, such as boats running aground or catching fire. But some mariners question whether the triangle could have been a factor in some of the shipwrecks, plane crashes and unexplained disappearances in the islands region.

"It's some kind of very strong magnetic force," Heinsen said. "The thing is, it's random. That's why most people can go through the Lake Erie Triangle and have nothing happen. But then somebody else goes through it, and they run into trouble."

Mysterious disappearances, such as people falling off boats or jumping into the lake and vanishing, only for their bodies to wash up on shore months later, and unexplained plane crashes have taken place in that area.

In December 1983, a Port Clinton police officer and four paramedics took off in a small plane from South Bass Island to Kelleys Island to help a man who was having a heart problems. The plane disappeared into a fog, and the wreckage and the men's bodies were found a few days later near the island, according to a UPI wire service story published on December 12, 1983.

The National Transportation Safety Board determined there were no mechanical failures that led to the crash and that the weather likely was the cause, the *Port Clinton News Herald* reported in an article published on December 9, 2016, about the anniversary of the tragedy.

In September 2007, a small, single-engine plane crashed on a clear night near Kelleys Island, killing a father and his nine-year-old son. An island resident in a rowboat rescued the crash's only survivor, the pilot's seven-year-old son, according to a *Toledo Blade* article published on September 5, 2007.

The NTSB found no evidence of any mechanical failure or malfunction, *General Aviation News* reported on September 24, 2009. The agency determined the crash was likely caused by the pilot having spatial disorientation, which is when a pilot cannot determine their true position and altitude in relation to the horizon.

A boat speeds in front of Kelleys Island, which is part of what some call the Lake Erie Triangle. *Kristina Smith.*

There are few historical accounts of the triangle. In December 1976, the Associated Press published a story about a diver, John O'Rourke, who referenced the triangle but also said he did not believe it had any sort of unusual force.

O'Rourke, who also taught at Wilmington College in Wilmington, Ohio, pointed out that at the time, there were as many "unusual" air and water disappearances per square mile in Lake Erie as there were in the Bermuda Triangle.

"He discounts the 'mysterious' properties of most disappearances, both in the Great Lakes and the 'Triangle,' tracing them to weather conditions, natural or human causes," according to the article, which was published on December 2, 1976, in the *Chillicothe Gazette.*

The following year, Jay Gourley published the book *The Great Lakes Triangle*, which suggested there was a triangle covering most of the Great Lakes, including Lake Erie, that was plagued with mysterious disappearances and accidents involving boats and planes, with reports of instruments not working.

Heinsen used to give ghost walks of the lakeside town of Port Clinton, where she lives and owns a bed-and-breakfast, and she included the Lake

Erie Triangle on the walk. Several of the walkers were familiar with the triangle and volunteered some of their own experiences.

Most described feelings of disorientation and fear. Their boat compasses and other navigational instruments often stopped working.

"I can remember some women saying, 'I never liked that area. I never liked it out there,'" she said. "There's something out there. I would say that it's just that whole atmosphere over the water, in the water."

"GHOST" SHIPS OF OHIO

At the northern and southern edges of Ohio, near some of the state's most heavily used ports, are two "ghost ships."

These boats are ghosts in that they sit abandoned and rotting, their disheveled and ominous appearances giving the impression a specter could be hiding in a cabin or that something awful happened on their decks.

Though they have not been the sites of grisly crimes or house hauntings, the histories behind these vessels are interesting in their own right.

Moored on the Black River just below the Lofton Henderson Memorial Bridge in Lorain, a city about thirty miles east of Cleveland on Lake Erie's shore, sits the *Upper Canada*, a steel ferry that has been abandoned for more than a decade.

Rust covers the ferry, which has an upper deck for passengers and carried cars on its bottom level. Its white lifeboat appears to be in surprisingly good shape, although plants are growing inside it. The white letters of the ship's name, *Upper Canada*, on the boat's side are faded but still legible.

The shoreline next to the boat is mostly undeveloped and covered in high grass and brush, and the entire area gives off an eerie, time-forgotten vibe, contrasted by the heavy traffic on the bridge above it. It's a sad state for a boat that took countless passengers to islands in Lakes Erie, Ontario and Huron.

The *Upper Canada* was built in 1949 by Russell Brothers Ltd. in Owen Sound, Ontario, according to BGSU's Historical Collections of the Great Lakes.

Russell Brothers kept an archive of its ships, and it includes several articles and records regarding the history of the *Upper Canada* through the years. The ship started out as the *Romeo & Annette*, and it was one of two ferries built for Captain Romeo Allard, who ran a ferry service between Bathurst, New Brunswick, and the Gaspe Peninsula in Quebec. The ship could hold twelve cars and forty passengers.

Today, the *Upper Canada* is moored on the Black River in Lorain, Ohio. *Kristina Smith.*

"The crossing is made in 15 minutes, which, considering it saves a 60 mile highway trip, is a fast service," the *Steelcraft News* reported in November 1949.

In 1965, the ship was sold to the Ontario Ministry of Transportation and renamed the *Upper Canada*. It served as a ferry between Kingston, Ontario, and Wolfe Island, which is part of the Thousand Islands between Ontario and New York State, until 1975.

In 1977, the ship began offering ferry service between Kingsville, Ontario, and Pelee Island, the largest of the Lake Erie Islands. Just before Christmas that year, the ferry was attempting to pick up the last load of winter fuel for the season at Kingsville Harbor to take to Pelee Island when it and a privately owned oiler got stuck in the lake ice.

The crews of both boats spent a frigid night on the frozen lake, and the U.S. Coast Guard sent an ice boat to rescue them in the morning. The ferry then was put up for the winter and started taking passengers to the island again in the spring. It operated there until 1991.

The boat's next stop was Lafontaine, Ontario. There, the *Upper Canada* again ferried people to an island, this time to Christian Island in Georgian Bay on Lake Huron. In 2000, the boat was retired and sent to Leamington, Ontario, to be stored.

The *Upper Canada* ferry during its days of taking passengers across the water. *Historical Collection of the Great Lakes at Bowling Green State University.*

How the *Upper Canada* ended up on the Black River is somewhat of a mystery. Al Johnson took ownership of the boat in 1999 and was its last recorded owner, BGSU records show. The ferry's vessel registration was suspended in 2008.

The ship, which appears to be stuck in mud under the water line, sits alongside property owned by 1284 Realty Co. Inc., Lorain County Auditor's Office records show. Alan Johnson of Avon, Ohio, incorporated the company with the State of Ohio in February 2000, according to Ohio Secretary of State records. Whether Alan Johnson of the realty company and Al Johnson, the boat owner in 1999, are the same person couldn't be confirmed.

The Lorain Port Authority receives inquiries about the ferry now and then, especially during the summer, when kayakers and boaters are active on the river, said Kelsey Levya-Smith, a port authority office manager. Over the years, the U.S. Coast Guard and Army Corps of Engineers have examined the boat and determined it is not leaking any materials and is not a navigation hazard.

"There's no harm being caused to the environment around it because of the boat being there," Levya-Smith said. "It's not blocking the right-of-way for boat traffic. Because of that, I think the owner has been able to kind of park it and leave it there for years without having anything done to it."

Those curious to see the boat more closely can take one of the port authority's shuttle cruises along the river, which passes the *Upper Canada* and includes some history about the ferry.

Much like the *Upper Canada*, another ship with perhaps an even more storied career is beached in disrepair near the southern end of the state.

The *Sachem*, also known previously as the *Celt*, USS *Sachem SP-92*, USS *Phenakite PYc-25*, *Sightseer* and *Circle Line V*, is run aground in Taylor Creek, a small tributary of the Ohio River, at Petersburg, Kentucky, not far from Cincinnati.

The ship was a racing and luxury yacht, served in both world wars, became an experimental lab for Thomas Edison and was even featured in one of Madonna's music videos.

The *Sachem*'s first name was the *Celt*, and its story began in 1901. Wealthy Manhattan businessman John Rogers Maxwell had the steam yacht built in Wilmington, Delaware, by the Pusey and Jones Company, a major boat builder at the time, according to the Sachem Project's website.

The *Celt* was the flagship of Maxwell's racing fleet, and he sailed it frequently around the city and Long Island Sound. The craft was opulent,

The ferry's lifeboat still appears to be in good shape, although weeds have started to grow inside it. *Kristina Smith.*

The ferry's name is still visible, although quite faded. *Kristina Smith.*

fitting for a wealthy man who regularly played host to boating excursions and wanted to impress his guests.

The deck houses and nine staterooms were lavished with carved mahogany woodwork, and adjoining bathrooms featured mosaic tiled floors. Each stateroom had a wardrobe, dressing table, icebox and other accessories, as well as plumbing and electricity.

"This vessel was the toast of the whole New York coastline for nearly a decade," according to the Sachem Project.

After Maxwell died, the yacht's next owner was another wealthy businessman, who renamed it *Sachem*. When the United States entered World War I in 1917, the U.S. Navy began seeking private boats for the war effort, because the speedy yachts could outmaneuver German U-boats.

Sachem joined the Navy on July 3, 1917, and became the USS *Sachem SP 192*. During the war, Thomas Edison used it as a floating laboratory to conduct experiments on various technologies he hoped would help with the war effort. The Navy, however, never produced any of the ideas he came up with while working on the boat.

After the war, the USS *Sachem* became the *Sachem* again and was used as a charter fishing boat until 1941, when the United States entered World War II. The Navy again drafted the ship for the war effort, this time renaming it

USS *Phenakite*. It was assigned to Key West Harbor in Florida and patrolled the East Coast between Long Island Sound and the Florida Keys.

After World War II, the ship again returned to recreational uses. It offered sightseeing cruises around New York City and was aptly renamed *Sightseer*. The boat was remodeled to carry 492 passengers, and for over thirty-one years, it showed nearly 3 million tourists around the city. During that time, the company that owned it renamed it two more times: *Circle Line Sightseer* and *Circle Line V*.

By 1977, the ship's best days were over. It was partially dismantled and essentially scrapped in the mud of the Hudson River in New York.

Then in the mid-1980s, Cincinnati-area businessman Robert "Butch" Miller took an interest in the boat, bought it, returned its name to *Sachem* and painted and restored it. Every weekend, he drove to Bayonne, New Jersey, where he docked the boat, to work on its restoration. While there, one of pop singer Madonna's representatives saw the boat and asked if it could be used in the background of the music video for Madonna's "Papa Don't Preach" in 1986.

The video was perhaps the last hurrah for the ship. Miller decided to bring it to Ohio, and in 1988, he embarked on a forty-day voyage with his wife, a few friends and a dog. The boat traveled down the Hudson River, through the Erie Canal, across the Great Lakes, into Chicago, down the Mississippi River and into the Ohio River.

Miller docked the boat next to property he owned on Taylor Creek. Over the years, water levels receded, stranding the boat in the creek mud. He eventually ran out of money to fix it.

Miller sold the land and moved to Mexico. He died in 2016.

In recent years, a group of the boat's former crew members, maritime historians and people living in the Cincinnati area started the Sachem Project and were working to raise money to restore the storied yacht. Attempts to reach them were unsuccessful. The Sachem Project website was last updated in 2018.

PART III

UFOs AND MYSTERIES

OF THE SKY

11

THE PORTAGE COUNTY
UFO CHASE

In the early morning hours of Sunday, April 17, 1966, a handful of police officers in Ohio and Pennsylvania had an experience that would forever change their lives. Portage County Sheriff's Deputy Dale Floyd Spaur and his partner, Wilbur L. "Barney" Neff, were driving in their police cruiser, patrol car P-13, through the countryside near the town of Randolph when a call came over their radio.

Around 5:00 a.m., Mrs. Harry Hays of neighboring Summit County called law enforcement to report a light in the sky that was "too high for a street light and too low for an airplane." Spaur, a thirty-three-year-old former Air Force gunner, later recalled that he and his partner initially laughed at the early radio chatter. As he told the *Akron Beacon Journal*, "I have always been a science-fiction fan, but I never believed in flying saucers."

By that point in 1966, newspapers across the United States had been publishing articles about "flying saucers" and strange lights in the skies for months. Three weeks earlier, U.S. House Minority Leader Gerald Ford had publicly called for a formal congressional inquiry into unidentified flying objects (UFOs) after numerous sightings that spring had left his constituents in southern Michigan concerned.

Spaur and Neff resumed their patrol near Randolph when they spotted a 1959 white Ford abandoned along Route 224. As the pair investigated the empty car, they noticed a light rising from a patch of woods to their south. They told the *Beacon Journal* the light moved directly toward them, and they fled to their cruiser. "It was so bright you couldn't even look up at it. It was like looking at a welder," Spaur said.

According to Spaur, the "intense" light hovered directly over their car for about two minutes while they sheltered in place. Then the object rose one thousand feet straight into the air, at which point they were able to get a better look at it. Spaur told reporters he saw a dome-shaped metallic object with a flat bottom and no wings. He figured it was about forty feet in diameter across its base and twenty feet tall. A beam of light emanated from the bottom of it toward the ground, and some kind of "antenna" protruded fifteen feet downward from its base. Spaur also said the object made a humming sound as it hovered.

At the same time Spaur and Neff said they were under the object, Mantua Police Chief Gerald Buchert called into the police station to report a strange light visible from his home in Mantua. He even had the foresight to grab his camera and snap a photograph. He estimated the object was hovering over State Route 224 about twenty miles to his south in Randolph. "It was like a moving star, only it didn't twinkle," Buchert told the *Akron Beacon Journal* the following day. The newspaper also reported that this same light was "spotted by hundreds" across the region.

UFO LOOKED LIKE THIS — Portage County deputy sheriff Dale Spaur indicates that the shape of a flying object he chased early yesterday looked like the head of a flashlight! Spaur and his partner, W. L. Neff, said they drove 86 miles following the object through eastern Ohio before losing it near Conway, Pa. "Somebody had control over it," Spaur said. "It can maneuver." (AP Wirephoto).

Dale Spaur demonstrating to reporters what the object looked like. *From the* Mansfield News Journal.

Portage County Sheriff's Deputy Robert Wilson, who was working the radio and listening to Spaur's updates, suggested that Spaur pull out his .44 pistol and take a shot at the object, but their sergeant thought it best not to "agitate" it. Spaur was instructed to stay put until a camera car could arrive to document incident.

Before the camera car could arrive, the UFO began to drift eastward. Spaur and Neff began to follow it in their police cruiser. As they accelerated, so did it. The deputies clocked their speed at 103 miles per hour, and they struggled to keep pace with it. Spaur noted that at one point, they took a wrong turn and had to double back to cross a bridge, only to find the object waiting for them. "It dropped to an altitude of 500 feet and stopped and waited for us when we got tangled up," Spaur told the *Beacon Journal*. "When we got on the road again, it started moving again."

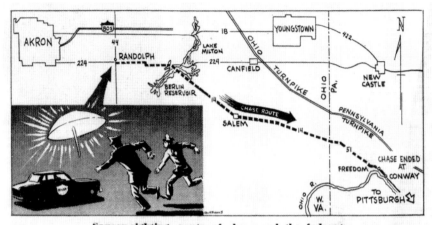

Saucer-sighting, route of chase and the fadeout.
By Beacon Journal Artist Byron Fairbanks

The route of the Portage County UFO chase. *From the* Akron Beacon Journal.

As the deputies broadcast updates over the radio, Patrolman H. Wayne Huston from East Palestine, a town along the Ohio-Pennsylvania border, spied the incoming object and joined the chase.

The growing convoy of Ohio police cars crossed into Pennsylvania and continued to pursue the elusive object another twenty miles until Spaur and Neff's car began running low on gas. They pulled into a gas station in Conway, Pennsylvania, and watched the object from their car as it ascended straight up until it disappeared out of view. A fourth officer, Frank Panzanella from the Conway Police Department, arrived at the gas station and said that he had also followed the object.

Wilson told reporters he had followed the ordeal over the radio for about fifty minutes and that the object was reported by six or seven police departments. He estimated the chase spanned some eighty-five miles. (Note: Initial newspaper reporting and nearly all subsequent literature claim the officers' pursuit covered eighty-six miles, but inputting the reported route into Google Maps yields a shorter distance of sixty-five miles.)

While many area residents reported what they saw to the local police, some called the United States Air Force. Within one day of the incident, the *Beacon Journal* noted the National Unidentified Aerial Phenomena Office (Project Blue Book) at Wright-Patterson Air Force Base in Dayton was opening an investigation.

What had started as a routine morning patrol on Sunday became international news on Monday. The public had been fascinated with flying saucer reports since the early 1950s, and from a journalistic perspective, this case was in many ways the ideal UFO sighting. It had dozens of witnesses, many of whom were in law enforcement. The United States Air Force was involved. And there was even a photograph. The Associated Press (AP) and United Press International (UPI) picked up the story, and it was carried in newspapers across the United States and Canada.

What became known as the Portage County UFO chase was one of the most widely covered flying saucer cases up to that point, with news outlets closely following its dramatic developments for several weeks. Many of those developments would overshadow the encounter itself.

One of the earliest controversies surrounding the incident involved the Buchert photograph. The *Beacon Journal* reported that the head of Project Blue Book, Major Hector Quintanilla, had advised Chief Buchert not to release the photograph to the press before the government could analyze the film. That claim was repeated by AP and UPI outlets, and it gave the government's investigation the air of a cover-up from the outset. In reality, Project Blue Book did request that Buchert mail the negatives to Wright-Patterson AFB for technical analysis, but Quintanilla told Buchert he was free to do whatever he wanted with his developed copies. The *Beacon Journal* published the grainy black-and-white photograph on April 19 under the headline "Here's a UFO."

The public waited eagerly for Project Blue Book's report over the next several days and pieced together what information they could in the meantime. The AP called the Federal Aviation Agency (today's Federal Aviation Administration, or FAA), which said no unusual objects were picked up on radar from air traffic control at the Greater Pittsburgh Airport (today's Pittsburgh International Airport). The *News-Reporter* in Hubbard, Ohio, sent a reporter to the nearby Youngstown Air Reserve Station to follow up on rumors that Air Force reserve training pilots had scrambled jets to chase the object, an assertion the station dismissed as false.

Multiple civilian UFO research organizations began their own field investigations of the event. The UFO Research Flying Saucer Investigating Committee of Akron scoured the site where the object was said to have hovered with a Geiger counter but failed to detect any radioactivity. The Pittsburgh Investigative Subcommittee of the National Investigations Committee for Aerial Phenomena (NICAP) sent one of its investigators, William Weitzel, to interview witnesses and monitor the government's investigation. That effort would culminate in a 138-page report published later that summer.

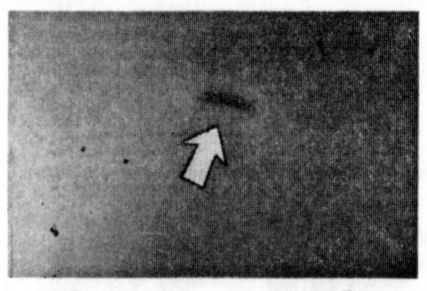

Here's A UFO

"The Buchert Photograph," taken by Mantua Police Chief Gerald Buchert and published in the *Akron Beacon Journal. From the* Akron Beacon Journal.

Project Blue Book released its official conclusion on April 22. "The object in the sky Deputy Sheriff Dale F. Spaur of Ravenna, Ohio, said he and his partner chased for 1½ hours last Sunday probably was the planet Venus," reported the AP. According to the Air Force, the deputies had seen a satellite reflecting the predawn light, and after it disappeared below the southeastern horizon, they picked up the bright planet Venus (visible in the morning in the spring of 1966) and continued the pursuit. The object in Chief Buchert's photograph, the Air Force continued, was a defect on the film negative that he produced as he attempted to take a picture of Venus.

The Air Force's dismissal sparked equal amounts of ridicule and outrage. While international headlines like "Ohio Officer Was Chasing Planet Venus, AF Claims" and "Police Chased Venus?" painted Dale Spaur as a fool who had pursued a planet across state lines, those who claimed they saw something remarkable that morning objected to Project Blue Book's statement. "They put out a lot of stories, the Air Force does," Portage County Sheriff Ross Dustman told the *Akron Beacon Journal* the following day. "Anyone is free to believe them. But I'll go along with my Deputies.... It was not a satellite and not Venus."

NICAP investigators raised serious questions about the accuracy and thoroughness of the Air Force's investigation. Still working on his report, Weitzel told reporters that "NICAP [had] uncovered a lot of information which refutes the Air Force's explanation" and that their explanation had "adversely affected the two deputies."

Residents around Northeast Ohio weren't buying Project Blue Book's satellite and Venus theory either. One resident from Massillon finally "yielded to temptation" and wrote a lengthy letter to the editor of the *Beacon Journal*, questioning, "Why does the Air Force seemingly try to make a monkey or a nitwit out of everyone who says he has seen a UFO?"

The Project Blue Book file for the case (Project 10073 Record), which was released to the public through the Freedom of Information Act and is now available online at the government document archive website the Black Vault, reflects a mostly superficial investigation on the part of the Air Force. While the file contains over ninety pages of material, the majority of those pages consist of newspaper clippings of the incident and nearly illegible black-and-white photocopies of Buchert's photographs.

The evidence collected by Project Blue Book, which informed its statement to the press, seems to consist of one witness questionnaire comprising thirty-five short questions that ask about the circumstances of the sighting and a handful of telephone calls made by investigators at Wright-Patterson AFB.

Despite redactions made to protect the privacy and identity of the witness, it is abundantly clear from the written comments that the person who filled out the questionnaire on the day of the sighting was Chief Buchert. Buchert indicated that for about ten minutes, he saw a "very bright white" light that appeared as a sphere at rest and changed shape to a plate that tilted forward when moving.

The day after Spaur reported his experience to Wright-Patterson, Air Force personnel called the Greater Pittsburgh Airport to determine that they had picked up nothing unusual on radar. The Air National Guard in Pittsburgh and Youngstown confirmed to Blue Book that F-102s had not been scrambled from either station. The Air Force then contacted Northwestern University to request wind data for northeastern Ohio, hypothesizing that the officers had perhaps spied a weather balloon, a possibility the data did not support. The majority of the investigators' telephone calls were made to national and local media outlets to learn what reports they were receiving from the area.

Major Quintanilla called Spaur twice on April 18 and 21. "The first one was about two and a half minutes, the second about one and a half minutes," Spaur said in a signed statement given to NICAP's William Weitzel on April 27. "Each time, the interviewer seemed to want me to say I had only seen the UFO a few minutes, because when I said how long I had seen it, he did not ask any further questions about my sighting." According to Spaur, Quintanilla opened their conversation with: "So, tell me about this mirage you saw."

From the beginning, Quintanilla had let it be known that representatives from the Air Force would not be conducting an in-person investigation, since, as he told the *Ravenna Record-Courier*, "it would be impossible to recreate the scene." This hands-off approach did not sit well with the people of Portage County or their elected officials.

Portage County Common Pleas Judge Robert E. Cook, a former congressman and veteran of the Air Force, took up his pen to write a letter to Congressman J. William Stanton, requesting a full, on-site investigation. "Their conclusion that the object sighted was the planet Venus is so ridiculous that the U.S. Air Force has suffered a great loss of prestige in this community," he wrote. "Wright-Patterson is not far away, and I am sure there are personnel available to conduct a thorough investigation."

Weitzel also wrote to Stanton, sending him a draft of his comprehensive report on the incident for NICAP. Weitzel provided transcripts of interviews he conducted with nine law enforcement officers who claimed they saw the object, detailed maps of each stage of the encounter and a review of Blue Book's analysis of the Buchert photograph, as well as radio dispatch logs from the Portage County Sheriff's Department and the FAA in Pittsburgh.

The public outcry persuaded Congressman Stanton to send a letter and a copy of the preliminary NICAP report to General John P. McConnell, the chief of staff of the Air Force, requesting that Project Blue Book perform a more thorough investigation in his district. "I'm a firm believer that if there is something the Air Force wants to hide, they are making a very big mistake. If they want the support of the American people they should above all be honest," Stanton told the *Ravenna Record-Courier* on May 5. "If they don't know, they should tell us—but to say there is nothing...I can't buy that!"

Weitzel noted that Stanton's letter to the Air Force went unanswered. Undeterred, the congressman visited the Pentagon in person and spoke with Lieutenant Colonel John Spaulding, the director of community relations for the Air Force, and demanded the case be reopened. A reluctant Quintanilla arrived in Ravenna the following week on May 10.

A sketch drawn by Dale Spaur for NICAP investigator William Weitzel. *National Investigations Committee on Aerial Phenomena.*

Hector Quintanilla Jr. had been investigating UFOs for the Air Force for nearly three years when the Portage County UFO chase occurred. He had immigrated to the United States from Mexico at the age of six and discovered he had a knack for math and science during his high school years.

He was studying physics at St. Mary's University in San Antonio when his draft notice arrived in 1943. Quintanilla studied radio and radar through the U.S. Army Air Corps before he was sent to the South Pacific as part of the Air Force's Seventy-Second Bomb Squadron.

After the war, Quintanilla returned to civilian life, became a naturalized American citizen and finished his physics degree. However, a return to military life called to him. He was commissioned as a second lieutenant with the Air Force in 1951 and spent the next decade stationed in Germany, Japan and Italy.

In the spring of 1963, Quintanilla received a phone call from Lieutenant Colonel Robert Friend, Project Blue Book's director since 1959, saying that he was being reassigned stateside to Wright-Patterson. Quintanilla summarized his feelings on being selected to head up Project Blue Book in an unpublished 1975 memoir he titled *UFOs: The $20,000,000 Fiasco*: "I've often been asked, 'How did you get involved with flying saucers?' My answer has always been short and simple. I was appointed to the position by my superior officer." Though Quintanilla's recollections never went to print during his lifetime, his manuscript was published electronically by the National Institute for Discovery Science, an organization founded by billionaire and UFO enthusiast Robert Bigelow, under the title *UFOs: An Air Force Dilemma* in 2016.

When he arrived in Ravenna, Quintanilla first distributed questionnaires to Spaur and Neff, who recounted the same story they had relayed to the press two weeks earlier. Their questionnaires are now preserved along with Chief Buchert's in Project Blue Book's file on the case.

Joining the officers' statements is a fourth questionnaire that was sent to Wright-Patterson on April 23. It came from an unidentified woman in Vandalia, Ohio, a suburb of Dayton, over two hundred miles away. She stated that in the predawn hours of April 17, she had seen a point of light rise from the west, arc overhead and disappear to the northeast. Her testimony seems an odd inclusion for an alleged police pursuit from the other side of the state—but for a handwritten note in the margin: "SATELLITE."

Quintanilla gathered Deputies Spaur, Neff and Wilson and Sheriff Dustman at the Portage County Courthouse for an interview. Officer Huston from East Palestine and Officer Panzanella from Conway, Pennsylvania, were unable to attend. Spaur had felt distrustful of the Air Force, which he believed had maligned his intelligence and character when it released its conclusion to the media, so he requested that NICAP record the interview for "back-up." Weitzel transcribed the tape recording and included it in his final report.

THE STAFF OF PROJECT BLUE BOOK — as the Air Force calls its UFO investigation—is headed by Major Hector Quintanilla, Jr. (seated). Others on his staff are (left to right) First Lieut. William F. Marley, Jr., Staff Sgt. Harold T. Jones, Mrs. Hilma Lewis, typist, and Mrs. Marilyn Stancombe, secretary.

Major Hector Quintanilla and the staff of Project Blue Book. *From* Philadelphia Daily News.

In the beginning of the interview, Quintanilla listened as Spaur and Neff described how they could "very clearly" see a metallic object roughly the size of a "three-bedroom ranch home" that performed "beautiful maneuvers." The object, they claimed, took up the "top better third of the windshield" when it was at its lowest, "and everything was lit up—it was real bright."

After the officers recalled their experience, Quintanilla asked for Weitzel and another NICAP representative to leave the room. "When you gentlemen first saw this thing," he began once they were alone, "how low was it on the ground?"

Quintanilla had Spaur and Neff walk through their story again from the beginning. He let Spaur go on for several minutes until the deputy reached the point in the tale where all "four officers, standing side by side," heard

Pittsburgh air traffic control on their radio discussing scrambling fighter jets and "could see these planes coming in."

"There were no fighter planes that were scrambled," Quintanilla objected. "The radar didn't pick anything up, and that's why no aircraft were scrambled." He explained that no sources could corroborate the officers' testimony that fighter jets from Pittsburgh or Youngstown had been scrambled or even that any air traffic conversation about the object had occurred at all. He went on to describe how he had determined that no weather balloons or classified military balloons had been operating in that area at the time either.

From the transcript, it appears Quintanilla then tried to convince Spaur that he and the other officers had seen an Echo satellite. "I checked with them [the monitoring stations]," he said. "The only thing that they had over this particular area was satellite Echo. I don't know whether you realize it or not, but there are at least thirty satellites that are visible to the naked eye. And these things have a northeasterly and southeasterly component."

Shortly after the Soviet launch of *Sputnik I* in 1957, engineers from the United States Air Force and Bell Telephone Laboratories started thinking about how orbital satellites could be used to relay communications signals around the curvature of the earth. Project Echo was officially launched by the newly formed National Aeronautics and Space Administration (NASA) in 1959, with the goal of putting large, reflective Mylar balloons laminated with aluminum foil into orbit to bounce radio signals off their surfaces to receivers stationed elsewhere on the globe.

The project's first passive communications satellite, *Echo 1*, did not achieve orbit, but its immediate successor, *Echo 1A*, reached space in 1960. In 1964, NASA successfully launched a second satellite, *Echo 2*. The pair remained in decaying orbits for several years before finally reentering the atmosphere in 1968 and 1969, respectively.

Echo 1A and *Echo 2* were inflated metallic spheres that measured 100 and 150 feet in diameter, respectively, and they orbited between 650 and 1,000 miles above the Earth. Despite their incredible distance from the Earth, the reflectivity of these "satelloons" made them easy to spot in the night sky. Many local newspapers regularly published the schedule for Echo flyovers in their weather section. For example, on April 27, 1966, the *Zanesville Times Recorder* printed that *Echo 2* would be passing over eastern Ohio from north to south from 3:15 to 3:35 a.m., and *Echo 1A* could be seen an hour later from 4:40 to 5:00 a.m., traveling southwest to northeast. To give a modern perspective, the International Space Station, a popular object for sky

A static inflation test of a Project Echo satellite. *National Aeronautics and Space Administration.*

watchers, is nearly three times larger than *Echo 2* and maintains a much lower orbit, at an altitude of only 250 miles.

"And this is why I made the determination specifically," Quintanilla continued, "because of the directions which you gave me. That you had first spotted the satellite coming over, and then focusing on Venus. Venus at that night, that's a typical night, was at a magnitude of -3.9, which is the brightest thing in the sky, except for the moon."

Project Blue Book's records indicate that Quintanilla was not being truthful with the deputies. Personnel from Wright-Patterson made phone calls two weeks earlier on April 29 to NASA's Goddard Flight Center and Marshall Space Flight Center, as well as the Smithsonian Astrophysics Laboratory, to inquire if there had been satellites from Project Echo or Project Pegasus, another NASA project studying the effects of micrometeoroid impacts on spacecraft, above eastern Ohio at that time. While the organizations told Blue Book officials they had stopped tracking the three Pegasus satellites the previous year, they said it was "definitely not *Echo 1* or *Echo 2* [as] they were over the southern hemisphere at the time of the sighting."

Even though Spaur was unaware that Quintanilla knew it was impossible for the officers to have pursued an Echo satellite, he grew increasingly agitated at what he saw was an attack on his mental stability. "I have [Neff] with me, we're going down the road; so you're gonna discount, well, there's two nuts! We're running Venus....I have hallucinations then!"

"I didn't say you were having hallucinations," said Quintanilla as the pair began talking over one another. "I'm not calling you a nut. I'm not saying you had hallucinations."

After Spaur again explained that he didn't chase Venus, Quintanilla said calmly, "You know, Dale, for whatever it's worth, you're not the first one it's happened to." He then explained that the Air Force had over ten thousand reports of "misinterpretations of conventional objects and natural phenomena" on file at Wright-Patterson.

Sheriff Dustman, who had been mostly quiet during the meeting, protested that Quintanilla was not listening to his deputies' testimony. "I'm like Dale. Nobody will ever convince me it wasn't something actual that's up there," he concluded.

"Sheriff, it's been unpleasant," began Quintanilla—remarking for the second time how "unpleasant" his job as a Blue Book investigator was— "but I've checked all the activity. This is one of the reasons I stayed home so I could check all the activity. Because it's a lot easier for me check with my communications channels, sit and just punch buttons, and say, 'OK, get me Akron, get me Cleveland, get me Toledo.' And then check out the information."

After the two-hour-long meeting, Weitzel recorded an exit interview with a frustrated Spaur and Neff. "I think his mind was made up before he come up here," Spaur said. "I think this was, to my estimation, a pacification of politicians. I think this was a way to show they come up for an interview to be done with it permanently. I think this was a way to write it off the books to satisfy skeptics or whatever the case might be....I know this thing was there. I personally don't give a damn who does or doesn't believe it. I'm not going to change one word of what I said."

Neff left the meeting, put off by the "insinuations" from Quintanilla. "He'd say one thing and then turn right around and say he didn't say it. 'I never said that,'" Neff said. "He would lead us to believe we were having hallucinations and then when we ask him about it, why he'd say, 'No.'"

Before returning to Wright-Patterson, Quintanilla told the *Akron Beacon Journal* that he hadn't uncovered anything during his on-site investigation to reverse his previous conclusions and that the deputies could have seen "any one of five satellites of the more than 30 satellites that are in orbit."

An exasperated Weitzel wrote to Congressman Stanton the following day to thank him for his efforts in getting Project Blue Book to visit Portage County and to report on the "incredible performance" displayed by Quintanilla. "Not only did [Quintanilla] reiterate his original satellite-Venus explanation of the UFO sighting, but he tried to talk us into it," Weitzel wrote. "He left the impression that he had come only to satisfy certain demands for his physical presence in the area, and that he had brought his conclusion with him. It appeared to be a complete waste of time, on his part and on ours."

Weitzel's letter to Stanton, as well as copies he sent to Congressmen Gerald Ford, James G. Fulton and J. Edward Hutchinson, received only boilerplate responses. Weitzel sent Stanton two additional multipage letters in May and June, lobbying for a more thorough investigation of the Portage UFO chase, to which Stanton finally replied by commending Weitzel on the "fairness and broadness of your own personal investigation." Stanton assured him that he had done everything he could by forwarding the full NICAP report and their correspondence to the Air Force and calling Secretary of Defense Robert McNamara to recommend that independent scientists be included in any future UFO programs.

Unlike many of the alleged supernatural encounters profiled in this book, the UFO chase is not one that has been widely adopted by the communities of Portage County. But its lasting legacy can be found in the lives of those who experienced it, as well as in its influence on the field of ufology itself.

Over the summer of 1966, the news cycle moved on from the Portage UFO story. However, a few reporters tried to periodically keep tabs on the witnesses.

Writing that October, a staff writer for the *Akron Beacon Journal* named John de Groot found a much less talkative Chief Gerald Buchert. Buchert, who would continue to serve as Mantua's chief of police until his death in 1986, laughed "nervously" when de Groot called him. "It's something that should be forgotten…left alone," he said. "I saw something, but I don't know what I saw." Years later, another reporter, Mary Scheier, attempted to follow up on de Groot's leads for the AP in 1972 but couldn't get Buchert to talk about the UFO chase whatsoever.

Wilbur Neff wouldn't even speak with either reporter, but his wife told de Groot in 1966, "I hope I never see him like he was after the chase.…People made fun of him afterwards. He never talks about it anymore. Once he told me, 'If that thing landed in my backyard, I wouldn't tell a soul.' He's been through a wringer." Neff finally spoke publicly on the issue decades later in 2004, when he told *Cleveland Scene*'s James Renner, "I don't look up anymore. I look down. I just want to forget."

Amid intense media coverage, Conway's patrolman Frank Panzanella had his telephone disconnected when de Groot tried to speak with him, but he did open up years later once things had settled down. When Scheier spoke to him in 1972, Panzanella had recently lost his position with the Conway Police Department after he was exposed as being part of a racketeering scheme (for which he was later convicted). He told her that the uncertainty of the incident no longer bothered him. "I saw something that morning, but I don't know what."

De Groot was able to track down H. Wayne Huston, the officer who had joined the case in East Palestine. He had resigned from the force in the months following the incident, moved across the country to Seattle and was driving a bus under a new name, Harold W. Huston. "Sure, I quit because of that thing," he said. "You couldn't put your finger on it, but the pressure was there. The city officials didn't like their police officers chasing flying saucers." He didn't even pick up the phone when Scheier tried to call him, and he told Renner decades later that he just didn't want to talk about it.

A good explanation for the officers' tight lips can be found in the tragedy that enveloped Dale Spaur in the months and years after the event. Writing under the headline "Flying Saucer Blasts His Life," de Groot described interviewing a "bitter, lonely" Spaur, who had lost forty pounds and was living in a motel, surviving on cereal and cigarettes. Spaur was no longer a sheriff's deputy. He was making eighty dollars a week as a painter. His wife filed for divorce after he shook her hard enough to leave bruises. He served a brief stint in jail for domestic violence, and he hadn't seen his children in weeks.

Spaur blamed everything that had happened to him in the previous six months on the UFO. "If I could change all that I have done in my life," Spaur told de Groot, "I would change just one thing. And that would be the night we chased that damn thing." He had since taken to calling the UFO "Floyd" (Spaur's middle name), and he claimed it had appeared to him again on at least one occasion.

Despite the summer lull in public interest, de Groot's piece ran in the AP and was carried in newspapers from Tallahassee to Tacoma. An outpouring of public sympathy reached Spaur in the weeks that followed.

One fifteen-year-old student in Alabama mailed him her entire allowance of two dollars. An anonymous "working gal" sent sixty dollars to help the man who was suffering "the thoughtless harassment of the press and TV people." Many of Spaur's donations came from UFO experiencers who shared their own stories.

An uplifted Spaur, who had booked a speaking engagement to share his story with the Goodyear UFO Society for November, commented, "People really do care, don't they?" Nearly two hundred people turned out to see him speak. He even began work on a book titled *P-13*, though he never finished it.

In the years that followed, Dale Spaur became a recluse. The *Akron Beacon Journal* couldn't locate him in 1969, and his former friends said they'd lost contact with him. Similarly, Scheier wrote in 1972 that Spaur had "vanished," just like the flying saucer. Spaur's name briefly appeared in 1975, when he was sentenced for drunk driving. The crime report listed him as then living in his hometown of Ansted, West Virginia.

Akron Beacon Journal reporter Bob Von Sternberg finally tracked Spaur down in 1977, eleven years after the UFO chase. "I'll go to my grave before I change my story," the forty-five-year-old Spaur said before recalling his struggles over the previous decade. Spaur lived as a drifter, sleeping in motels when he had work and on the street when he frequently didn't. Getting called into the boss's office to collect his last paycheck had become routine for him: either the state had found him for back child support, or the company had figured out they'd hired a "nut" who saw flying saucers. Despite all its ups and downs, Spaur's life was coming back together. He remarried in 1975, moved home, reconnected with his mother and started a taxi service business with his new wife.

With respect to his unique reputation, Spaur told Sternberg that he had moved to Florida briefly in 1970, enticed by a reporter who'd hinted he could get a book deal from his story, a prospect that went nowhere. During the 1970s, Spaur's case became quickly became a favorite in paranormal circles, and the UFO enthusiasts annoyed him. "I grew a beard, put on some old work clothes and went to some of the UFO meetings. I sit there and hear people tell complete lies about me," he said. "These yo-yos talk about how they know you and the real story. They don't accomplish anything."

The Portage County UFO chase even impacted Major Quintanilla, who was arguably the cause of much of Dale Spaur's misery. Quintanilla recalled the case as a "shame" in his memoir. "I drove back to Wright-Patterson [from Ravenna] with an ominous feeling. I didn't like what was happening to

Dale Spaur and yet I was powerless to help him," he wrote. "The proponents of extraterrestrial visitation had used Dale Spaur and he wasn't aware of it."

Quintanilla's experience with those "proponents" led him to rethink the way he managed Project Blue Book after the Portage County incident. Since 1949, Dr. J. Allen Hynek, a professor of physics and astronomy at the Ohio State University, had served as scientific consultant for the Air Force's UFO programs that preceded Blue Book, Projects Sign and Grudge. A credible scientific voice and a UFO skeptic, Hynek often found prosaic explanations for reported UFO sightings. Captain Edward J. Ruppelt, the first director of Project Blue Book, brought Hynek into the program in 1953, because unlike many scientists, he didn't "give you the answer before he knew the question." But after investigating UFOs for several years, Hynek had become convinced that the phenomena was real and grew more vocal that the issue deserved greater consideration from the military.

Quintanilla saw the chase on April 17, 1966, as "the incident which convinced [him] Dr. Hynek was a liability." After releasing Blue Book's conclusion, the press, NICAP, sympathetic members of Congress and a handful of UFO-believing academics began exerting pressure on Quintanilla to change his evaluation. Even though Hynek had not been called on to investigate the case, enough people had demanded Quintanilla consult him that he reluctantly sent Hynek the Project Blue Book and NICAP reports. According to Quintanilla, Hynek advised that Blue Book would be wise to change its conclusion, because the case was "politically hot." On the other hand, it should be noted that Hynek maintained years later that he had submitted a "strong 'unidentified'" scientific evaluation, which Quintanilla rejected.

After the Portage County UFO chase, bad blood between the Air Force officer and the astronomer persisted for the rest of the decade. "It's ironical," wrote Quintanilla, "that in 1966 Dr. Hynek recommended that I be replaced and in the end I held the option whether to retain him or get rid of him. I didn't wish to retain him, so I just never invited him back." Hynek's consulting contract expired in 1969, shortly before Project Blue Book closed its doors. Now a leading figure in ufology, the former government contractor founded the Center for UFO Studies in 1973.

Dale Spaur's story has since become a classic in ufology and is frequently retold in paranormal literature. Hynek covered the Portage incident in great detail in his 1972 book *The UFO Experience: A Scientific Inquiry* where he called it the one case that "not only brings to a focus the nature of the Close Encounter phenomenon but also stands on record as an example of the ludicrous manner in which Project Blue Book sometimes went about investigating a case."

This case was, in many ways, a Holy Grail for UFO researchers, perfectly primed for a long life as a legend. It featured numerous witnesses from different vantage points. Most of those witnesses were law enforcement officials who are often considered more credible than civilians. It was well-documented. And lastly, the government's response smacked of a cover-up, which, for many, was proof enough that something extraordinary had indeed traversed the skies over Portage County.

Quintanilla's abrupt investigation already seemed suspicious to many observers, but Spaur himself infused the story with even more conspiratorial undertones when he spoke to de Groot in October 1966. He stated that when he and Neff had stopped to examine the abandoned '59 Ford just before they first saw the object, they discovered the car was filled with all kinds of strange radio equipment. Even stranger, Spaur now claimed, was that painted on the Ford's side was a triangle emblem with a lightning bolt emblazoned across it, along with the words: "Seven Steps to Hell."

The symbol that most closely matches Spaur's description (sans the lightning bolt) is the military emblem for the United States Seventh Army, an armored corps formed during World War II and commanded by George S. Patton. In 1966, during the Cold War, the Seventh was stationed in Germany as part of the United States' European Command.

Historic shoulder patches from veterans' uniforms depict a blue triangle containing the profile of a yellow seven-stepped pyramid, which signifies the Seventh's official motto: "The Pyramid of Power." Unofficially, soldiers of the Seventh adopted another slogan: "Seven Steps to Hell."

This is the first documented instance of Spaur ever mentioning the mysterious symbol. It was not reported in any press that spring, he never mentioned it in his interview with Major Quintanilla and it doesn't appear in the NICAP report. In fact, Weitzel wrote that the owner of the Ford was later discovered, with no mention of anything out of the ordinary on their car.

It is unclear why Spaur would suddenly include this peculiar detail six months after the fact—that is if the emblem was even painted on the car at all. Regardless, the ominous symbol and its loose connection to the military provided an excellent mystique. Within weeks of de Groot's interview, one particularly pious reader opined to his local newspaper that flying saucers were "Heaven's Omnipotent Untouchables" and that the cryptic symbol "connotes[s] Man's seven capital sins against Heaven."

One recent "alternative news" conspiracy theory website cites the Portage County UFO chase as evidence that this army unit, based in Germany, was tracking or perhaps even testing advanced craft made from Nazi technology in Ohio.

One of Spaur's children from his first wife, James Evans, has also contributed some of the legend's more fantastical lore. In a 2006 interview, Evans told James Renner that his father had once fallen down a mine shaft and was left in a coma. His attending nurse came "running out of his room, screaming" that "[Spaur's] body was possessed by an alien." According to Evans, Spaur laid comatose but had his eyes open (coma patients very rarely open their eyes) in the hospital for several days. But apparently, he experienced a "miraculous recovery."

According to Renner, Evans even remembered slews of strangers showing up to his father's funeral, including a group of Inuit whom none of the Spaur family recognized. He recalled the service, which he said was held shortly after his father "died on April 4, 1983," as being particularly odd. However, Dale Floyd Spaur's obituary in the *Cleveland Plain Dealer*, his grave marker and death records indicate he died on May 8, 1984.

Today, few outside of the UFO community remember the once-famous Portage County UFO chase. But millions have seen it indirectly immortalized by none other than Steven Spielberg.

Spielberg had shown an interest in UFO sightings beginning in his childhood, and some of his earliest projects as a fledgling filmmaker, such as *Firelight* in 1964, center on UFO investigations. After the success of *Jaws*, Spielberg began working on a novel and movie, both titled *Close Encounters of the Third Kind*, which were loosely based on J. Allen Hynek's *The UFO Experience*. In fact, Hynek developed the three-tiered "close encounters" system in order to classify UFO reports based on the witnesses' supposed level of contact with unidentified craft and their occupants. Spielberg hired Hynek to work as a consultant on the film, and Hynek even made a cameo during the iconic final scene, when the UFO lands at a government base.

Hynek, who was particularly fond of the story of the Portage County UFO chase, encouraged Spielberg to include an homage to the incident in *Close Encounters*. In one scene, the film's main character, Roy Neary, played by Richard Dreyfuss, sees several UFOs pass by overhead and begins chasing them in his truck. Several police cruisers join the high-speed pursuit down the Indiana Toll Road until the glowing craft eventually ascend into the sky and disappear. Neary becomes obsessed with his UFO experience, and that obsession wrecks his life. As one contemporary reviewer of the film wrote, "The untold story, however, is that this is exactly what happened to the real Deputy Spaur."

When the film was released in November 1977, *Close Encounters* set new box office records and won several awards. Furthermore, the film ushered in a new wave of public interest in UFOs. The film is remembered today as one of Spielberg's masterpieces and is considered by ufologists to be one of the most "accurate" on screen portrayals of the UFO phenomena.

The Portage County UFO chase can also be seen as a template for the resurgence of interest in UFOs that emerged in the late 2010s and 2020s (at the time of this writing). This new era for UFOs, renamed Unidentified Aerial Phenomena (UAP), began after it was revealed in 2017 that the Department of Defense had quietly resumed investigating UFO sightings, decades after Project Blue Book officially ended.

Like Dale Spaur and his fellow police officers, the witnesses who are coming forward to the press are often military personnel and are frequently referred to as "trained observers." Many of these modern witnesses, like Navy Commander David Fravor (retired) and Lieutenant Commander Alex Dietrich (retired), who both claim to have interacted with a UAP while flying jet aircraft off the coast of California in 2004, say that those who see strange things in the sky have their careers threatened by overwhelming stigma from their peers and superiors.

Today's UFO investigators, much like NICAP's William Weitzel in 1966, criticize the government's overreliance on mundane objects, like balloons and drones, to explain sightings. Ex–government insiders, like Luis Elizondo, reportedly the former director of the Pentagon's Advanced Aerospace Threat Identification Program, have spun their credentials into careers as vocal advocates for "UFO disclosure," much like Hynek did after his time with Blue Book.

Lastly, proponents of the "extraterrestrial hypothesis" have successfully lobbied members of Congress, such as Senators Marco Rubio and Kirsten Gillibrand and Representative Mike Gallagher, to push Defense Department officials to take the UAP issue more seriously and to be more transparent with the public, just as they did with Gerald Ford and J. William Stanton half a century ago. To date, these efforts have yielded a handful of public "UAP Reports" from the Office of the Director of National Intelligence beginning in 2021, a nationally broadcast congressional hearing on UAPs in 2022, and an interagency scientific panel on the subject livestreamed by NASA in 2023.

The Portage County UFO chase is one of the best documented stories from Ohio's paranormal heritage, even though its legend has expanded over the decades. While researchers will never know what those police officers saw on April 17, 1966, their story remains compelling because of the factual, real-world effect it had on the people involved. There is no doubt this Buckeye State legend will live on to fascinate new generations for as long as people continue to look up and ask, "Are we alone?"

12

THE WOW! SIGNAL

In August 1977, astronomer Jerry Ehman was sifting through dozens of printouts of jumbled numbers and letters representing radio signals picked up by Ohio State University's radio telescope.

As he pored over what to the untrained eye would seem like meaningless gibberish, he found something unusual from the August 15 printout: the sequence 6EQUJ5. Overcome with excitement, Ehman wrote "WOW!" in red pen next to the sequence.

Ehman had just discovered what many consider the best evidence of a potential alien radio contact with Earth ever found.

Today, the signal—dubbed the WOW! signal after Ehman's note on the printout—is still regularly cited by those who believe there is intelligent life beyond Earth.

But scientists and others who have studied it, including Ehman himself, are skeptical. They caution that it is most likely a blip or something explainable by nonalien life.

Even if the signal came from extraterrestrial beings, it was sent millions or billions of years before the telescope recorded it and translates into a long scream, said Don Stevens, an astrophysicist and director of Perkins Observatory in Delaware, Ohio. The observatory is located near the spot where the Big Ear radio telescope stood.

No matter where it originated, the WOW! signal has its place in history. It is carefully preserved at the state archives and library at the Ohio History

Center in Columbus, and staff are asked to bring it out now and then for documentaries and TV shows interested in what it might mean.

"It's one of those things where it encourages people to actually delve into science and learn more about astronomy and radio astronomy," Stevens said. "If it's something inspirational, great. The claim that the source is an extraterrestrial intelligence is just something that needs to be taken with a grain of salt and with healthy skepticism."

The Big Ear

To know what the WOW! signal is, one needs to understand the radio telescope, named the Big Ear, and Ohio State's search for extraterrestrial intelligence program, known as SETI.

The Big Ear was a radio telescope that took up about the same square footage as three football fields and had a massive antenna and receiver. It was built in the late 1950s and began listening to the sky in the early '60s, according to newsletters from North American Astrophysical Observatory, a nonprofit organization that was formed to support the Big Ear.

It was designed by Big Ear director and Ohio State professor John Kraus, PhD, and was built on Ohio Wesleyan University's property in Delaware, just north of Columbus. Ohio State's electrical engineering department ran the Big Ear.

It was "a monstrous thing, the most massive set of bedsprings you've ever seen in your life," according to the September 1987 NAAPO newsletter. "Imagine a giant Serta Sleeper measuring 100 feet in height and 300 feet in length or roughly the area of three football fields. Now imagine it tilting up and down to follow Earth's rotation."

Originally, it was built for national defense to track Soviet Union satellites and for radio astronomy, Stevens said. Later, the Big Ear was repurposed to scan the universe for any sounds that could be coming from intelligent life in the universe.

"It had a multichannel receiver, but it was very limited on the number of channels and frequencies it could listen to," Stevens said. "Mostly, what it would observe was whatever passed into what's called its beam. It was staring basically at a slice of the sky. As the Earth rotates, things would rotate in and out of its beam."

The Big Ear recorded what it heard in numbers on an IBM computer that spat out the pages of printouts that Ehman and others would review.

The Big Ear radio telescope was the size of about three football fields. *Courtesy of the Ohio History Connection, call number MSS1151AV.*

Each column on the printouts represented a radio signal from a different frequency, and the numbers and letters represented the relative strength of the signal, Stevens said.

At the time Ehman found the WOW! signal, the Big Ear was the largest radio telescope operating in the United States and the longest-running SETI program in the country, according to the archives at the Ohio History Center.

The goal of the SETI program was to find scientific proof of life beyond Earth. The Big Ear would listen to a range of frequencies, called the water hole, where it was transparent to certain radio wavelengths that some scientists believe extraterrestrial intelligences would use to communicate over interstellar distances.

"Water is very good at absorbing and scattering parts of the electromagnetic spectrum," Stevens said. "However, there are some gaps that allow the signals to reach the surface and therefore can be picked up by radio telescopes."

"It was thought that anyone that wanted to communicate would choose these frequencies," he said. "It's basically making an assumption that any intelligent life up there thinks like we do and wants to tell others that they're out there. There's a lot of assumption to that."

Still, the Big Ear team was confident that extraterrestrial life exists and that, perhaps, the Big Ear could prove it.

"As the saying goes, absence of evidence in not necessarily evidence of absence," Robert Dixon, the Big Ear's assistant director, said in the January 1987 issue of the NAAPO newsletter. "We may not receive a signal in my lifetime—perhaps not for a thousand years. That does not mean we should be discouraged."

Dixon and his colleagues, however, struggled to gain acceptance for their work in the scientific community and a steady funding stream for their research, NAAPO newsletters archived at the Ohio History Center show.

What Exactly Is the WOW! Signal?

When Ehman, who taught in Ohio State's Electrical Engineering Department and volunteered at the Big Ear, found the WOW! signal, *Star Wars: A New Hope* was still in movie theaters, and *Close Encounters of the Third Kind* would be released a few months later. The WOW! signal became, and remains today, a pop culture phenomenon.

It has been featured in documentaries, TV shows, social media videos and printed publications. The signal and Ehman were even referenced in a 1994 episode of the TV show *The X-Files*, titled "Little Green Men."

A scan of the printout with Ehman's handwritten red "WOW!" is requested so much that the Ohio History Connection has a specific procedure for obtaining permission to use it on its website, along with the information about the signal.

Despite the signal's fame, most don't really understand what it is, Stevens said.

"It was a burst of radio energy," Stevens said. "It was a strong peak during that period of observation. Mostly what you see throughout the printout is the relative background, just kind of the general noise of the universe and local environment. And then whatever caused that peak, when it rotated into the field of view, was picked up by the telescope."

The WOW! signal is often described as if it contains a message for Earth. Stevens, however, said the sequence doesn't spell out anything specific and that it is equivalent to a long scream.

"There was no coherent pattern to it," he said. "There was no information contained in it."

The signal was in the telescope's beam for seventy-two seconds. At that time, the radio telescope did not have audio recording equipment, so there is no audio of the signal, according to NAAPO's memorial website for the Big Ear.

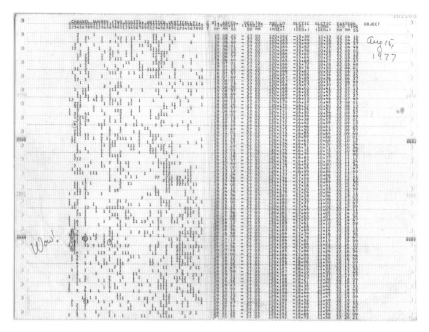

Jerry Ehman was so excited about the sequence he found from the radio telescope printout that he wrote "WOW!" in red letters on the scan. *Courtesy of the Ohio History Connection, call number AL07146.*

If it were an extraterrestrial sound, it originated from a time long before Ehman received it—perhaps millions to billions of years before the Big Ear picked it up, Stevens said.

"Radio signals are a kind of light, and they travel at the speed of light," Stevens said. "In terms of the universe, there is no such thing as now."

WHAT COULD HAVE MADE THE SIGNAL?

After determining the significance of the WOW! signal, Big Ear scientists used the timing of the telescope's rotation and where it was tilted at the time the signal came in to determine the approximate spot from which it originated. They then searched the area with optical telescopes and listened again with the Big Ear.

"They never found anything," Stevens said. "There is a star nearby but not exactly at the coordinates. They focused the radio telescope on that, but they never picked up anything."

Radio telescopes also can be problematic, because they pick up noises of all kinds, including those generated here on Earth, he said.

"Here on the ground, we have to worry about light pollution, radio pollution, cellphones, computers, vehicles and engines," he said. "Now, most radio observatories have an established radio quiet zone."

Anything from a malfunctioning toaster oven to a satellite or a black hole consuming a star could have created the WOW! signal, Stevens said.

Healthy skepticism doesn't mean Stevens, Ehman and others who study the sky don't believe extraterrestrial life is out there.

"Oh, I want it to be a signal from an extraterrestrial civilization," Ehman acknowledged to the *Columbus Dispatch* on June 27, 2010.

They are scientists first, and they must take a scientific view of the information from the Big Ear, Stevens said.

"We want to find intelligent life," Stevens said. "We want to answer the question: are we alone in the universe? We just don't make the leap from something that's culturally been misunderstood to 'there's life out there.' To think that we're the only intelligent life in the universe is preposterous because the universe is so big, and there's so much out there. Until we know, the only answer we can give scientifically is 'we don't know.'"

Big Ear Ends, but Research Continues

The WOW! signal has never been repeated, nor has any other signal like it been recorded.

Dixon and his team at the Big Ear fought for years to keep their research going, even as a developer tried to take over the telescope's land to expand its golf course in 1983, according to the NAAPO newsletters.

By September 1987, the Big Ear was mostly run by volunteers. NASA pitched in $15,000 a year to help operate it, and that, along with whatever money the staff could come up with in donations, was spent on technical expenses and stipends for graduate students, according to the September 1987 NAAPO newsletter.

"The personnel to run the program are provided by a consortium of colleges and universities who each contribute a faculty member and recruit students to serve in volunteer posts," according to the newsletter article. "The volunteers take care of literally everything from mowing the lawn to analyzing the data."

A month later, the golf course again became a threat. Ohio Wesleyan University was planning to sell the land that housed the Big Ear to the golf course developer.

The colleges and universities whose graduate students, staff and volunteers supported the Big Ear started a publicity campaign that included writing letters to President Ronald Reagan and famed astronomer Carl Sagan.

They sold three hundred T-shirts that said "Help Save Big Ear—E.T. May be Calling" and showed the telescope with the words "I'm sorry, that number is no longer in service," according to the October 1987 NAAPO newsletter.

Ohio State signed a lease with the new landowner, fending off the developer and continuing the Big Ear's research for another decade. As 1997 neared, however, Ohio State did not renew the lease.

In August 1997, twenty years after Ehman found the WOW! signal, Dixon and the other scientists at the Big Ear celebrated the anniversary with a party, complete with a WOW! signal cake, a viewing of the original printout and tours of the telescope, the October 1997 NAAPO newsletter reported.

The Armstrong Air and Space Museum in Wapakoneta has a case that includes some small pieces of the Big Ear radio telescope and information about the WOW! signal. *Kristina Smith.*

As 1997 ended, the Big Ear stopped listening. In 1998, it was demolished.

The golf course was expanded. Today, a lake covers the ground that once housed the Big Ear. A historical marker that shares a brief history of the Big Ear stands along the driveway to the golf course.

Some of the Big Ear's remains are housed at Perkins Observatory, which has a room with some of the telescope's equipment and a scale model of the Big Ear.

Some small pieces of the Big Ear are also on display in a small case at the Armstrong Air and Space Museum in Wapakoneta, Ohio. Greg Brown, the museum's historian and collections coordinator, described the case as a "minor curiosity" for the museum's visitors. He, too, believes the signal was an anomaly.

Still, SETI research continues elsewhere in the United States. Using radio telescopes and other technology, the SETI Institute in Mountain View, California, continues to search for evidence of extraterrestrial life.

"Confirmation of alien life is going to be a difficult thing," Stevens said. "It would also be one of the most profound things in human history if we achieve it."

13

THE COYNE UFO INCIDENT

Four U.S. Army Reserve officers had just passed their routine physicals in Columbus and boarded their helicopter to return to Cleveland on October 18, 1973.

They took off around 10:30 p.m. The night was calm, starry and moonless. The temperature was forty-three degrees, and visibility was good.

They were about seven miles east of the Mansfield Airport and Military Base and flying at about 2,500 feet over the woods, farms and rolling hills of central Ohio.

Suddenly, the crewmen in the back noticed a steady red light keeping pace with the helicopter. They thought it was an airplane until they realized the craft was bearing down on the helicopter so fast that a crash was imminent.

Taking immediate action to avoid collision, the pilot, Captain Lawrence J. Coyne, quickly put the helicopter into a dive of about five hundred feet per minute and contacted the Mansfield control tower to ask about jet traffic in the area.

But none of the communication channels were working. The radio was dead.

The craft emanating the red light hovered above the helicopter, and the crew described it as cigar-shaped and gray. It was silent.

At its nose was the red light, and at its tail was a white light. A green light beamed from the bottom and filled the helicopter cockpit with an eerie green glow.

After hovering over the helicopter for a few seconds, the cigar-shaped craft changed course and sped off. Although Coyne had lowered the helicopter's altitude, the helicopter had inexplicably risen one thousand feet during the encounter. Its compass was spinning.

The crew continued to Cleveland Hopkins International Airport without further incident. The men's lives, however, were forever changed.

And their experience, commonly known as the Coyne UFO incident, is considered one of the most credible and well-documented sightings of an unidentified flying object on record.

The Investigation

After the crew landed, Coyne felt he needed to report the incident to some sort of agency, but he didn't know of any that handled UFO sightings—neither did the Federal Aviation Administration.

So, Coyne shared what happened with his second cousin, who worked at the *Cleveland Plain Dealer* and wrote an article about the event. Although the story captured the public's attention, it didn't spark any interest from official agencies. Coyne then filled out an operational hazard report with the State Adjutant General's Office, which is a branch of the national guard.

The Center for UFO Studies in Evanston, Illinois, became interested and conducted a full investigation. CUFOS was founded by J. Allen Hynek, whose past work included being an astronomer at Ohio State University and the chief scientific consultant for Project Blue Book. By the time of this incident, Project Blue Book had been shuttered.

Hynek and Jennie Zeidman, a CUFOS investigator who worked with Hynek at Ohio State and on UFO cases for Project Blue Book, interviewed the crew. Hynek spoke with the pilot in January 1974, and Zeidman's interviews with Coyne and the rest of the crew took place two years later.

Zeidman headed up an investigation that lasted for years and documented her findings in a book, *A Helicopter-UFO Encounter Over Ohio*, which CUFOS published in 1979.

Zeidman, who lived in Columbus, located witnesses who saw the incident unfold from the ground and pored over reports and news articles related to the incident. She also considered and dismissed natural phenomena, such as a meteor, being responsible for the strange encounter.

"She was in a perfect position to investigate it, and she was a great investigator," said Mark Rodeghier, PhD, the president and scientific director of CUFOS who worked with Zeidman on other cases.

"LIKE LOOKING INTO ANOTHER WORLD"

Sergeant John Healey was the first to notice the strange light just before 11:00 p.m., according to Zeidman's book. He was sitting in the left rear seat of the helicopter.

Although the light seemed brighter than that of a normal plane, he didn't think much of it and didn't say anything. A few minutes later, Sergeant Robert Yanacsek, who was sitting in the right-rear seat, noticed the light as well and thought it seemed to be keeping pace with the crew's helicopter.

He told Coyne, who told him to "keep an eye on it," according to Zeidman's book. Thirty seconds later, Yanacsek saw the light closing in on the helicopter.

At this point, Coyne could see the light. The fourth crew member, First Lieutenant Arrigo "Rick" Jezzi, had an obstructed view due to where he was sitting in the copilot's seat.

"It was obvious that it was coming at us," Yanacsek told Zeidman. "We were positive it was going to intercept us, especially since the object or whatever it was had turned in our direction to begin with."

Although the helicopter crew had previously been speaking with the Mansfield Airport tower on the radio, communication went dead. Coyne radioed in, but there was no response on any channel. That's when Coyne put the helicopter into a dive to avoid a collision.

"We were going down in altitude, and it looked like it was still coming at us—it was descending in altitude also," Coyne told Hynek. "It was coming to wipe us out, you know?"

The cigar-shaped, metallic craft hovered above the helicopter, and the helicopter's compass began spinning. It never worked properly again and had to be replaced.

As the craft slowed and hovered above the helicopter, none of the crew felt the helicopter climbing in altitude, nor did they feel any turbulence or hear any sound, according to Zeidman's book.

The UFO's light bathed the helicopter in a green glow, although the crew members also reported the helicopter's windows were already tinted green to avoid glare from the sun during day flights. Healey got up and stood in the aisle between Coyne and Copilot Jezzi and watched the craft.

"It damn near came to a stop right over us," Healey told Zeidman. "So, we all got a very good look at it. It had no windows that we could see."

Suddenly, the craft made a forty-five-degree turn, sped off toward Lake Erie and disappeared. Coyne's and Yanacsek's accounts were consistent

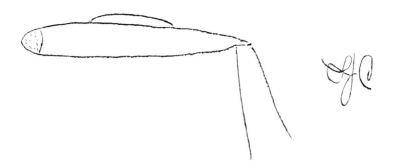

Captain Lawrence J. Coyne drew this sketch of the UFO he and the other military men in his helicopter saw. *Center for UFO Studies.*

with Healey's, and Coyne and Yanacsek drew identical sketches of the craft. Jezzi, who was able to see the object as it hovered above the helicopter, also gave the same account.

"All hell broke loose in the cockpit," Jezzi told Zeidman. "Everybody was starting yelling and screaming about what the hell it was and that it almost hit us."

Healey told his cousin a year after his interview with Zeidman the same story and said he thought the craft wanted to get a closer look at the helicopter, according to Zeidman's book.

"He was curious like we were curious, but he had the ability to outrun us," Healey is quoted as saying to his cousin in Zeidman's book.

The incident, which Zeidman estimated, based on the interviews, lasted five minutes, shook all four of the crew members. For Healey, the scariest part was how quickly the craft appeared, came to a stop to hover over the helicopter and sped off.

Over dinner with Hynek, Coyne said watching the craft hover above them was "like looking into another world," according to Zeidman's book.

Ground Witnesses

Nearly two years after the incident, a group of central Ohio residents interested in UFOs, known as the Civil Commission for Aerial Phenomena, put out a call for witnesses to the Coyne incident in the *Mansfield News Journal.*

One of the people who came forward was a woman who said she and the four children riding with her in her car that night saw what happened. She contacted Warren Nicholson, the organization's director. He and Zeidman interviewed the group.

The woman, identified only as Mrs. C, left her mother-in-law's home in Mansfield at about 10:40 p.m. with her three children and another child, who was an extended family member, for her home in rural Ashland County, not far from Mansfield.

The children were Charles, thirteen; Camille, eleven; Curt, ten; and an extended family member named Karen, thirteen. The group said they saw a single steady red light that was very bright flying at about the speed of a jet before it disappeared, according to Zeidman's book.

As the family turned onto Ohio 430, they saw the craft again, but this time, it had a red and green light. It was flying low over the Charles Mill Reservoir. They noticed the craft was slowing and seemed to stand still.

Mrs. C pulled the car over, and the family saw and heard the military helicopter approaching. Charles and Karen got out of the car for a better look. The group saw the object and the helicopter converge.

Charles said the UFO was a blimp-shaped object that projected a bright green light.

"It was so bright that you couldn't see too far," he told the investigators. "Everything just turned green. I think the green came from above the helicopter. It kind of looked like rays coming down."

Then the helicopter passed over them, and the UFO was above it, projecting the green light, Charles told investigators. Then the UFO disappeared.

In 1988, two more witnesses came forward to Zeidman when she was at the Richland Mall in Mansfield, manning a CUFOS photograph exhibit. Jeanne Elias, in her fifties at the time of the mall visit, and her son, John, twenty-nine, approached her, according to an article Zeidman wrote for the November/December 1988 edition of *International UFO Reporter*, published by CUFOS.

The pair, who lived in Mansfield near the Charles Mill Reservoir, reported hearing a helicopter flying over their house. Jeanne, who was in bed, put her head under the pillow when she heard the noise. She said the helicopter was so close it sounded like it might crash into the house.

John, who was fourteen at the time of the incident and also in bed, came into her room and asked her if she had seen the green light.

"The green light lit up the room," John told Zeidman. "It seemed like it took a few minutes. At least long enough for me to wake up and see it and hear it."

Landmark UFO Case

Today, the Coyne UFO incident remains one of the most credible and evidential incidents of a UFO encounter, Rodeghier said. There are many reasons it has stood the test of time.

First, the credibility of the men in the helicopter was excellent, Rodeghier said. They were all military members with reputable backgrounds.

Coyne, the pilot, was a full-time commander of the 316 Medivac Unit in the U.S. Army Reserve and a former plainclothes officer for the Cleveland Police Department. He was thirty-six at the time of the incident.

Coyne also described himself in a story by wire service UPI that was published in newspapers across the country that he was a UFO skeptic until the incident and wasn't sure what to make of it, according to the version of the story that ran in the *Indianapolis Star* on November 4, 1973.

Jezzi was the copilot and a chemical engineer. This was his first flight with the rest of the helicopter crew. He was twenty-six at the time.

Healy was a flight medic and a detective for the Cleveland Police Department's Intelligence Unit. He was thirty-five at the time.

Yanacsek was the crew chief and an IBM service representative. He served in the Vietnam War as a helicopter crew chief. He was twenty-three at the time.

Of the four men, Yanacsek was the only one who reported having a previous experience with a UFO. While flying a helicopter at night in Vietnam, he saw three white lights flying in tight formation, and they passed beneath his helicopter. The lights didn't appear to be attached to anything, he told Zeidman.

"Over the year and a half I worked with the aircrew, there was never any indication of collusion, hoax or willful exaggeration," Zeidman wrote in her book.

Coyne was so shaken that he reported the incident to the FAA's chief of operations at Hopkins Airport in Cleveland, P.J. Vollmer, the day after it happened. Hynek also interviewed Vollmer, who thought Coyne was credible.

"In a case of this kind, I don't know anybody that I would believe any more," Vollmer told Hynek. "I trust his judgment without a question or a doubt."

In addition to the crew's detailed accounts of the incident, there were witnesses to the event on the ground.

"Secondly, it wasn't just a light going by. Their helicopter seems to have been affected," Rodeghier said, referencing the unexplained climb of the helicopter's altitude, the broken compass and the failed radio communication.

"In principle, one of our own devices being affected by a UFO is not unheard of," he said. "But for planes, it's still very rare, which is, of course, why it was so dramatic an experience."

The incident was reported right away, and there were multiple witnesses.

"They were interviewed shortly after that and completed report forms," he said. "All of that makes it a very important case."

Lastly, this incident occurred during a wave of UFO sightings across Ohio and the entire eastern seaboard that remain unexplained, he said.

"Skeptics have attempted to explain this incident away and haven't been able to," he said.

COULD IT HAVE BEEN SOMETHING EXPLAINABLE?

The Coyne UFO case won the *National Enquirer* Blue Ribbon Scientific Panel $5,000 award for "the most scientifically valuable report of 1973," according to an article Zeidman wrote for *Fate Magazine*, a publication dedicated to the paranormal, in August 1978. Coyne and the crew received the money.

Journalist and UFO skeptic Philip Klass, however, opined that the crew should return the money, because there was a reasonable scientific explanation for the incident and the witnesses' stories didn't add up.

Klass, an electrical engineer, aviation publication editor and author of books suspicious of UFO reports and alien abduction stories, wrote several letters to Zeidman challenging her investigation. He and Zeidman published side-by-side conflicting explanations of the incident in *Fate* in December 1978.

Klass thought what the crew saw could have been a meteor or fireball from the Orionids meteor shower, which was near its peak intensity on the night of the incident, he wrote in his explanation.

He cited a letter he received from the director of the American Meteor Society, David D. Meisel, in January 1974. Meisel wrote that the Orionid meteor shower was especially known for its fireballs.

Further, Klass said a United Airlines pilot flying near Pittsburgh two nights after the Coyne incident reported seeing a meteor or fireball at 10:07 p.m.

"Fireballs characteristically have long, luminous tails of electrified air or plasma, which may extend for many hundreds of yards, and if this was indeed a fireball, the light from its long tail would have illuminated the cockpit for perhaps several seconds as it passed over the helicopter," Klass wrote.

Klass also challenged the credibility of the witnesses on the ground, saying the incident did not happen over the Charles Mill Reservoir, as they stated. He also argued that eyewitness accounts from two years after the incident were not reliable.

In a letter he sent to Zeidman in October 1978, Klass went as far as to ask Zeidman to have the mother of the children in the car who said they witnessed the incident take a lie detector test.

The dead radio could be explained by Coyne switching channels too quickly in his panic on seeing the light on a collision course with his helicopter. Or the Mansfield operator, presumably the only person on duty, could have been talking to someone else on another channel and missed Coyne's radio call.

And the strange ascent of the helicopter by one thousand feet could be explained simply by Coyne or Jezzi instinctively moving the controls to regain altitude and not realizing they had done it due to the adrenaline rush of a potentially dangerous situation.

Zeidman, however, examined and dismissed the possibilities of the UFO being a fixed-wing aircraft, helicopter or meteor.

The UFO the crew described didn't match the description of any fixed-wing aircraft or helicopter and would not have been capable of decelerating from such a high rate of speed to hovering, nor would it have been silent, she wrote in her book.

Additionally, Coyne checked with the FAA and found no record of any other aircraft in the area. The last-known F-100 from the Mansfield Air National Guard had landed at 10:47 p.m., about thirteen minutes before Coyne incident, Zeidman wrote.

No meteors were reported in the Mansfield area on the night of the incident, and a meteor would not have appeared as an opaque object that blotted out the view of stars, as the unidentified craft did.

Meteors last a few seconds, but this event lasted about five minutes, she wrote.

In letters Zeidman sent to others involved in UFO research in response to their request for her thoughts on Klass's comments, she expressed annoyance at Klass's assertions, saying that he had never met with Coyne in person or conducted extensive research, as she had, into the incident. She described one of his papers as "ludicrous," according to one of the letters, which are held in the CUFOS files.

Regardless of the debate, the incident remains unsolved. UFO researchers continue to point to it as one of the reasons UFO research should continue.

"At this point, UFOs are a scientific problem," Rodeghier said. "We believe that future historians will look back on this period since World War II, when UFO sightings became prominent, as a period of scientific blindness, where something was hitting us in the face and it was ignored by the establishment. No subject in science should be off-limits for study."

EPILOGUE

Years and sometimes more than a century after they originated, stories of creatures, UFOs and unexplained phenomena continue to persist and evolve. Whether the readers of this book believe in them or not, these legends of the Buckeye State touch their lives in one way or another.

U.S. Department of Defense officials testified before Congress in May 2022 about their review of UFO sightings, which the government rebranded as "unidentified aerial phenomena" (UAP) until 2023, when the term was further revised to "unidentified anomalous phenomena" in order to include the "aerial, space and undersea domains." The hearings were the first of their kind to be held in fifty years.

"UAP reports have been around for decades, and yet we haven't had an orderly way for them to be reported—without stigma—and to be investigated," Congressman Adam Schiff (D-California), chairman of the House Intelligence Committee, said in his remarks, as quoted by *Time* magazine on May 17, 2022. "That needs to change."

These hearings came after 144 reports of these UAPs, including some that military pilots caught on video in the 2000s, were declassified in June 2021. The Department of Defense and Congress's Intelligence Committee are perceiving these objects as potential threats to national security. The UAP issue has received a renewed sense of urgency in the wake of the United States shooting down a Chinese spy balloon and three unknown objects in North American airspace in February 2023. To date, the government's All-domain Anomaly Resolution Office is following up on over 850 reported UAP cases. This story will continue to evolve in the coming years.

Sightings of Bigfoot and other creatures persist around the country, and thrill seekers still visit the sites of popular urban legends for a good scare on a dark night.

TV shows about the paranormal, such as the "reality" shows *Finding Bigfoot* and *Ghost Adventures*, remain ever popular and have increased interest in the supernatural. Fictional shows, like *The X-Files* and *Supernatural*, usually take their inspiration from urban legends and popular ghost stories. The proliferation of streaming services has increased the number of movies and shows on these topics.

You can spend hours listening to podcasts about unexplained historical mysteries, aliens, creatures and other paranormal accounts and reading countless books on the same subjects.

Ghost tourism has become commonplace at historic sites across Ohio, especially around Halloween. The Licking County Historic Jail in Newark, Collingwood Arts Center in Toledo and Franklin Castle in Cleveland are all examples of allegedly haunted sites offering either guided tours or investigative ghost hunts. The most famous and successful paranormal attraction in the state is the Ohio State Reformatory in Mansfield, which often sells out its guided ghost walks weeks in advance. Ghost hunting groups gladly pay $100 per person for the opportunity to have the decrepit prison all to themselves.

As technology has changed, however, so has folklore.

The digital age is creating new urban legends and folklore. Some folklorists call this new genre Creepypasta, according to *I Know What I Saw* by Linda S. Godfrey. The term is a mashup of the word *creepy* and internet slang for "copy and paste" known as *copypasta*.

Those who create these new stories "copy" details from urban legends and tales that already exist and "paste" in their own creepy elements to create their own scary stories. Creepypasta.com is filled with frightening fan fiction tales.

Perhaps the best example of a new urban legend this genre has created is Slenderman. Eric Knudsen created this terrifying tall and skinny monster in 2009 for an online writing contest, and fans made their own mythos for it. The version of Slenderman that many recognize has no face and can teleport and instill horrible dreams and feelings of paranoia in his victims. Slenderman quickly went viral as an internet meme.

Despite Slenderman being a work of fiction, people began claiming they had encounters with it within a few years of its creation. Two twelve-year-old girls in Wisconsin claimed to be under the spell of Slenderman when

Slenderman. *Illustration by Kari Schultz.*

they stabbed their friend in 2014 in the woods. The victim survived, and the girls were found not guilty by reason of mental defect and institutionalized.

The tragic incident only added to the Slenderman story's notoriety. On paranormal radio shows and in online message boards like Reddit, Slenderman has since become affiliated with stories of spirits in Native American folklore that were believed to encourage people to do evil things.

In mainstream media, the TV show *Law & Order: SVU* in 2014 aired an episode that was loosely based on the case, and a book, *Slenderman: A Tragic Story of Online Obsession and Mental Illness*, which details the case, was published in 2020.

Creepypastas are the continued evolution of folklore in the digital age, albeit at an accelerated rate. Tales that used to take decades to develop now take only a few years to spread with the benefit of the internet. Future generations will likely look back on these online horror legends and glean insight into the fears of people today.

Perhaps in fifty years, these new Creepypastas will be the folktales told and retold for generations, just as the legends featured in this book have been.

BIBLIOGRAPHY

INTRODUCTION

Books and Publications

Bader, Christopher D., Joseph O. Baker and F. Carson Mencken. *Paranormal America: Ghost Encounters, UFO Sightings, Bigfoot Hunts, and Other Curiosities in Religion and Culture*. 2nd ed. New York: New York University Press, 2017.

Sims, Martha C., and Martine Stephens. *Living Folklore: An Introduction to the Study of People and Their Traditions*. Logan: Utah State University Press, 2005.

1. BIGFOOT

Books and Publications

Arment, Chad. *The Historical Bigfoot: Early Reports of Wild Men, Hairy Giants, and Wandering Gorillas in North America*. 2nd ed. Drake County, Ohio: Coachwhip Publications, 2019.

Newton, Michael. *Strange Ohio Monsters*. Atglen, PA: Schiffer Publishing Limited, 2013.

Renner, James. *It Came from Ohio…: True Tales of the Weird, Wild, and Unexplained*. Cleveland, OH: Gray & Company, Publishers, 2012.

Interviews

DeWerth, Marc (organizer of the Ohio Bigfoot Conference at Salt Fork State Park). Discussion with the author. July 22, 2022.

Hanks, Micah (founder of the Debrief and host of podcast *Sasquatch Tracks*). Discussion with the author. July 13, 2022.

Hickenbottom, John (naturalist for the Ohio Department of Natural Resources at Salt Fork State Park). Discussion with the author. June 13, 2022.

Newspapers and Periodicals

Akron Beacon Journal   Cincinnati Enquirer

Websites and Online Resources

Bigfoot Field Researchers Organization. www.bfro.net.

2. THE LOVELAND FROG

Books and Publications

Bloecher, Ted, and Isabella Davis. *Close Encounters at Kelly and Others of 1955.* Evanston, IL: Center for UFO Studies, 1978.

Freeburg, Jessica, and Natalie Fowler. *Monsters of the Midwest: True Tales of Bigfoot, Werewolves & Other Legendary Creatures.* Cambridge, MN: Adventure Publications, 2016.

Newton, Michael. *Strange Ohio Monsters.* Atglen, PA: Schiffer Publishing Limited, 2013.

Renner, James. *It Came from Ohio…: True Tales of the Weird, Wild, and Unexplained.* Cleveland, OH: Gray & Company, Publishers, 2012.

Stringfield, Leonard H. *Inside Saucer Post…3–0 Blue: Close Encounters of Many Kinds.* Cincinnati, OH: Civilian Research Interplanetary Objects, 1957.

Willis, James A., Andrew Henderson and Loren Coleman. *Weird Ohio: Your Travel Guide to Ohio's Local Legends and Best Kept Secrets.* New York: Sterling Publishing Company Inc., 2005.

Interviews

Rahe, Dennis Sean (chief of the Loveland Police Department). Email to the author. March 7, 2022.

Newspapers and Periodicals

Cincinnati Post   Gadsden Times
Dayton Journal Herald   ORBIT

Articles

Behind the Curtain Cincinnati. "HOT DAMN! IT'S THE LOVELAND FROG Review." May 30, 2014. https://behindthecurtaincincy.com/2014/05/30/hot-damn-its-the-loveland-frog-review/.

Dalea, Natalie. "The Strange Case of the Loveland Frog, Ohio's Amphibian Cryptid." Portalist. July 29, 2020. https://theportalist.com/the-loveland-frog.

Haupt, Ryan. "The Loveland Frog." *Skeptoid.* June 30, 2015. https://skeptoid.com/episodes/4473.

Hugo West Theatricals. "HOT DAMN! IT'S THE LOVELAND FROG: A Bluegrass Musical." https://hugowesttheatricals.wixsite.com/home/blank-2.

Kwin the Eskimo. "Classic Cryptid: The Legend of Ohio's Loveland Frogmen." *Week in Weird.* July 24, 2012. http://weekinweird.com/2012/07/24/classic-cryptid-legend-loveland-frogmen/.

Leggate, James. "Know the Legend of the Loveland Frogman? This Man Claims He Spotted It." WCPO. August 4, 2016. https://www.wcpo.com/news/local-news/hamilton-county/loveland-community/did-pokemon-go-players-encounter-the-legendary-loveland-frogman.

———. "Officer Who Shot 'Loveland Frogman' in 1972 Says Story Is a Hoax." WCPO. August 5, 2016. https://www.wcpo.com/news/local-news/hamilton-county/loveland-community/officer-who-shot-loveland-frogman-in-1972-says-story-is-a-hoax.

NICAP. "Leonard H. Stringfield—Who's Who in Ufology?" https://web.archive.org/web/20130912052144/http://www.nicap.org/bios/stringfield.htm.

Russell, Davy. "The Loveland Frog." *X-Project Paranormal Magazine.* March 1, 2001. http://www.xprojectmagazine.com/archives/cryptozoology/lovelandfrog.html.

Tyler. "Shawnahooc (Loveland Frog)." Shoggoth.net. October 15, 2014. https://shoggoth.net/octobernomicon/the-actual-creatures-of-the-octobernomicon/the-loveland-frog/.

Willis, James A. "Create Your Very Own Loveland Frog Hoax for Under $20.00!" *My Strange and Spooky World.* August 9, 2016. https://strangeandspookyworld.com/2016/08/09/create-your-very-own-loveland-frog-hoax-for-under-20-00/.

3. THE DOGMAN OF DEFIANCE

Books and Publications

Freeburg, Jessica, and Natalie Fowler. *Monsters of the Midwest: True Tales of Bigfoot, Werewolves & Other Legendary Creatures.* Cambridge, MN: Adventure Publications, 2016.

Renner, James. *It Came from Ohio…: True Tales of the Weird, Wild, and Unexplained.* Cleveland, OH: Gray & Company, Publishers, 2012.

Interviews

Blackburn, Lyle (author of books about cryptid creature sightings, producer of documentaries on cryptid creatures and guest on various TV shows that aired on Discovery and Travel Channel). Discussion with M. Kristina Smith. February 14, 2022.

McClary, Janet, and Kent McClary (hosts of the *Dead Air Paranormal* radio show). Discussion with the author. September 12, 2021.

Smith, Al (former reporter for the *Crescent-News*). Discussion with the author. February 14, 2022.

Newspapers and Periodicals

Defiance Crescent-News   *Orange Leader*
Lawton Constitution   *Toledo Blade*

4. SOUTH BAY BESSIE

Books and Publications

Freeburg, Jessica, and Natalie Fowler. *Monsters of the Midwest: True Tales of Bigfoot, Werewolves & Other Legendary Creatures*. Cambridge, MN: Adventure Publications, 2016.

Newton, Michael. *Strange Ohio Monsters*. Atglen, PA: Schiffer Publishing Limited, 2013.

Interviews

Gabriel, Tory (extension program leader and fisheries educator for Ohio State University's Ohio Sea Grant College Program and Stone Laboratory). Discussion with the author. September 15, 2021.

Popik, Ray (curator of the Greater Cleveland Aquarium). Discussion with the author. November 12, 2021.

Schaffner, John (publisher of the *Beacon* newspaper). Discussion with the author. October 29, 2021.

Newspapers and Periodicals

Associated Press   *Sandusky Register*
Los Angeles Times   *Sandusky Star-Journal*
Sandusky Daily Register

5. THE MELON HEADS OF KIRTLAND

Books and Publications

Freeburg, Jessica, and Natalie Fowler. *Monsters of the Midwest: True Tales of Bigfoot, Werewolves & Other Legendary Creatures.* Cambridge, MN: Adventure Publications, 2016.

Renner, James. *It Came from Ohio…: True Tales of the Weird, Wild, and Unexplained.* Cleveland, OH: Gray & Company Publishers, 2012.

Willis, James A., Andrew Henderson and Loren Coleman. *Weird Ohio: Your Travel Guide to Ohio's Local Legends and Best Kept Secrets.* New York: Sterling Publishing Company Inc., 2005.

Newspapers and Periodicals

Chillicothe Gazette

Cincinnati Enquirer

Detroit Free Press

East Liverpool Evening Review

Hartford Courant

Lansing State Journal

Livingston County Daily Free Press and Argus

Mansfield News-Journal

Port Huron Times Herald

St. Joseph Herald-Palladium

Articles

Bendici, Ray. "The Melon Heads." *Damned Connecticut.* https://www.damnedct.com/the-melon-heads/.

Bittar, Bill. "White Lady Ghost, Melon Heads, Annabelle among Monroe's Spooky Lore." *Monroe Sun*, October 31, 2021. https://themonroesun.com/white-lady-ghost-melon-heads-annabelle-among-monroes-spooky-lore/.

Cleveland Magazine. "CLE Myth: Our Favorite Spooky Urban Legends." November 25, 2019. https://clevelandmagazine.com/in-the-cle/articles/cle-myths-our-favorite-spooky-urban-legends.

Dimick, Aaron. "MICHIGAN MONSTERS: Beware of the Melon Heads of Saugatuck." WWMT. May 9, 2016. https://wwmt.com/news/local/michigan-monsters-beware-the-melon-heads-of-saugatuck.

Mangan, Dennis. "Years Ago | December 18th." WFMJ. December 18, 2019. https://www.wfmj.com/story/41470517/years-ago-or-december-18th.

Polansky, Rachel. "3News Investigates the 'Melon Heads' of Kirtland." WKYC. October 30, 2020. https://www.wkyc.com/article/life/holidays/halloween/3news-investigates-melon-heads-kirtland/95-31c66168-e6b3-4348-a7c6-7a34127b19eb.

Websites and Online Resources

Fox Funeral Home. "Dean F. Kroh Obituary." 2020. https://www.foxfuneralhomeinc.com/notices/Dean-Kroh.

Hydrocephalus Association. "20 Powerful Facts About Hydrocephalus." https://www.hydroassoc.org/powerful-hydrocephalus-facts/.

IMDB. "Legend of the Melonheads." 2010. https://www.imdb.com/title/tt1773538/.

———. "The Melonheads." 2011. https://www.imdb.com/title/tt2648138/.

John Hopkins Medicine. "Hydrocephalus in Children." https://www.hopkinsmedicine.org/health/conditions-and-diseases/hydrocephalus/hydrocephalus-in-children.

New England Historical Society. "The Melon Heads of Connecticut." 2022. https://www.newenglandhistoricalsociety.com/the-melon-heads-of-connecticut/.

Stanford Medicine Children's Health. "About Pediatric Hydrocephalus." https://www.stanfordchildrens.org/en/service/hydrocephalus/about#:~:text=Abnormal%20head%20size%2C%20sometimes%20too,mean%20a%20patient%20has%20hydrocephalus.

6. MOTHMAN

Books and Publications

Barker, Gray. *The Silver Bridge*. Clarksburg, WV: Saucerian Books, 1970. Reprint, Seattle: Metadisc Books, 2008.

Hasken, Eleanor Ann. "The Migration of a Local Legend: The Case of Mothman." PhD diss., Indiana University, 2022.

Keel, John A. *The Mothman Prophecies: A True Story*. New York: Saturday Review Press, 1975. Reprint, New York: Tor Books, 2002.

———. *Operation Trojan Horse*. New York: Putnam, 1970. Reprint, New York: Illuminet Press, 1996.

———. *Strange Creatures from Time and Space*. New York: Fawcett Gold Medal Books, 1970. Reprint, Point Pleasant, WV: New Saucerian Books, 2014.

Newton, Michael. *Strange Ohio Monsters*. Atglen, PA: Schiffer Publishing Limited, 2013.

Renner, James. *It Came from Ohio…: True Tales of the Weird, Wild, and Unexplained*. Cleveland: Gray & Company, Publishers, 2012.

Sergeant, Donnie, Jr., and Jeff Wamsley. *Mothman: The Facts Behind the Legend*. Point Pleasant, WV: Mothman Lives Publishing, 2002.

Steinmeyer, Jim. *Charles Fort: The Man Who Invented the Supernatural*. New York: Penguin Books, 2007.

Willis, James A., Andrew Henderson and Loren Coleman. *Weird Ohio: Your Travel Guide to Ohio's Local Legends and Best Kept Secrets*. New York: Sterling Publishing Company Inc., 2005.

Manuscript Resources

Keel, John. Personal notes and correspondence. http://www.johnkeel.com/.

Newspapers and Periodicals

Associated Press
Athens Messenger
Charleston Daily Mail
Charleston Gazette
Cincinnati Enquirer
Cincinnati Post
Coshocton Tribune
Dayton Daily News
Fort Worth Star-Telegram
Hartford Courant
Huntington Herald-Dispatch
Lancaster Eagle Gazette
Lewiston Evening Journal

Mansfield News Journal
Middleport Daily Sentinel
Montreal (Quebec) *Star*
Philadelphia Daily News
Point Pleasant Register
Raleigh Register
Saucer News
Southern Historical Journal
Springfield News Sun
United Press International
Weirton Daily Times
Wilmington News Journal
Zanesville Times Recorder

Articles

Allen, Emily. "Thousands Gather for Mothman Festival in Point Pleasant." West Virginia Public Broadcasting. Setpember 23, 2019. https://www.wvpublic.org/news/2019-09-23/thousands-gather-for-mothman-festival-in-point-pleasant.

Colavito, Jason. "Is the US Government Summonging Satan through UFOs?" *Jason Colavito Blog*. June 5, 2015. https://www.jasoncolavito.com/blog/is-the-us-government-summoning-satan-through-ufos.

Davis, Jeff. "Response to 1967 Disaster Created a Program That Has Gradually Lost Its Focus." *Transportation Weekly*, August 15, 2007.

Elbein, Asher. "Is the Mothman of West Virginia an Owl?" Audubon Society. October 26, 2018. https://www.audubon.org/news/is-mothman-west-virginia-owl.

Keel, John A. "World of Monsters: Awful Creatures in the Night." *San Francisco Examiner*, July 19, 1970.

Lavender, Dave. "Video Game to Be Based in a Post-Apocalyptic Mountain State." *Huntington Herald-Dispatch*, June 12, 2018. https://www.herald-dispatch.com/features_entertainment/video-game-to-be-based-in-a-post-apocalyptic-mountain/article_09ab293b-41aa-5b78-bed4-d880937ece7a.html.

O'Neill, Claire. "Welcome to the 'TNT Area,' Home of the Mothman." NPR. January 23, 2012. https://www.npr.org/sections/pictureshow/2012/01/23/145334460/welcome-to-the-tnt-area-home-of-the-mothman.

Plein, Stewart. "Gray Barker and the Men in Black: They Knew Too Much About Flying Saucers." *West Virginia University Libraries Blog*. May 25, 2021. https://

news.lib.wvu.edu/2021/05/25/gray-barker-and-the-men-in-black-they-knew-too-much-about-flying-saucers/.

Roadside America. "Mothman Statue." https://www.roadsideamerica.com/story/12036.

Sherwood, John C. "Gray Barker: My Friend, the Myth-Maker." *Skeptical Inquirer* 22, no. 3 (May/June 1998): 37–39.

———. "Gray Barker's Book of Bunk: Mothman, Saucers, and MIB." *Skeptical Inquirer* 26, no. 3 (May/June 2002): 39–44.

Slowik, Ted. "Chicago's 'Mothman' Stories Are Good Paranormal Entertainment." *Chicago Tribune*, July 29, 2017. https://www.chicagotribune.com/suburbs/daily-southtown/opinion/ct-sta-slowik-chicago-mothman-st-0730-20170728-story.html.

WSAZ Metro News. "15th Annual Mothman Festival in Mason County." WSAZ. September 17, 2016. https://www.wsaz.com/content/news/50-years-after-1st-reported-sightings-of-Mothman-hes-still-a-draw-in-Point-Pleasant-393848001.html.

Audio and Visual Resources

Fallout 76. Rockville, MD: Bethesda Softworks, 2018. XBox One.

Gulyas, Aaron. "A Cold Day in West Virginia." *Saucer Life*. Podcast aired December 19, 2018. https://storage.pinecast.net/podcasts/3ec5ea72-7da7-4f55-b872-86403c3b30ad/audio/5d8e7789-a640-4507-ad12-823cbc35ea11/encounter704acolddayinwestvirginia.mp3.

———. "John Keel and the Mothman Prophecies." *Saucer Life*. Podcast aired December 15, 2018. https://storage.pinecast.net/podcasts/3ec5ea72-7da7-4f55-b872-86403c3b30ad/audio/3443238a-8f79-4166-be41-76f5afc3008f/Encounter706JohnKeelandtheMothmanPropheciesPart1.mp3.

———. "Mothman Unplugged." *Saucer Life*. Podcast aired October 15, 2018. https://storage.pinecast.net/podcasts/3ec5ea72-7da7-4f55-b872-86403c3b30ad/audio/0ba47bc9-852d-4879-94e5-6f517ead5b06/encounter702mothmanunplugged.mp3.

———. "The Silver Bridge." *Saucer Life*. Podcast aired October 12, 2018. https://storage.pinecast.net/podcasts/3ec5ea72-7da7-4f55-b872-86403c3b30ad/audio/45103bf4-ee50-40c6-905e-916887e7074b/encounter703thesilverbridge.mp3.

MrBadSeed1976. "The Man Called Cold: The Woody Derenberger Interview [November 3, 1966]." YouTube video, 29:57. Posted September 10, 2012. https://www.youtube.com/watch?v=5HxY4suVjSo.

Pellington, Mark. *The Mothman Prophecies*. Culver City, CA: Sony Pictures, 2002. BluRay.

UllageGroup. "John Keel Interview with David Letterman [July 28, 1980]." YouTube video, 8:17. Posted April 10, 2013. https://www.youtube.com/watch?v=KC5f9OYSRa8.

Wilkinson, Bob. *Shades of Gray*. Seminal Films, 2009. DVD.

Websites and Online Resources

Environmental Protection Agency. "Criminal Provisions of the U.S. Criminal Code (Title 18) and Other Statutes—Migratory Bird Treaty Act of 1918." https://www.epa.gov/enforcement/criminal-provisions-us-criminal-code-title-18-and-other-statutes.

Mothman Festival. https://www.mothmanfestival.com/.

MothmanLives. http://mothmanlives.com/.

West Virginia Department of Transportation. "Silver Bridge." https://transportation.wv.gov/highways/bridge_facts/Modern-Bridges/Pages/Silver.aspx.

World's Only Mothman Museum. https://www.mothmanmuseum.com/.

7. The Elmore Rider

Books and Publications

Westropp, Thomas J. "The Death Coach." In *A Folklore Survey of County Clare*. London: Transactions of the Folk-Lore Society, 1910. https://www.clarelibrary.ie/eolas/coclare/folklore/folklore_survey/chapter3.htm.

Willis, James A., Andrew Henderson and Loren Coleman. *Weird Ohio: Your Travel Guide to Ohio's Local Legends and Best Kept Secrets.* New York: Sterling Publishing Company Inc., 2005.

Woodyard, Chris. *Haunted Ohio: Ghostly Tales from the Buckeye State.* Beavercreek, OH: Kestrel Publications, 1991.

Interviews

Harrison, Jeffrey (chief of Elmore Police Department). Email to the author. February 21, 2022.

Newspapers and Periodicals

Fremont News Messenger   *Port Clinton News Herald*

Articles

Astonishing Legends. "The Elmore Rider." October 6, 2019. https://www.astonishinglegends.com/astonishing-legends/2019/10/6/the-elmore-rider.

Atlas Obscura. "Elmore Tombstone Derby." November 2, 2015. https://www.atlasobscura.com/places/elmore-tombstone-derby.

Dray, Ashley. "Driving Down this Ohio Road Will Give You Nightmares." Only in Your State. https://www.onlyinyourstate.com/ohio/haunted-road-oh/.

Fringe Paranormal. "The Legend of the Elmore Rider." February 14, 2013. https://fringeparanormal.wordpress.com/2013/02/14/elmore-ghost-rider/.

Richardson, Mark. "The Headless Motorcyclist on Ghost Road." *Canada MotoGuide*, October 29, 2018. https://canadamotoguide.com/2018/10/29/the-headless-motorcyclist-on-the-ghost-road/.

Shoup, Craig. "Elmore Tours Get Up Close and Personal with Ghosts and Ghouls." *Port Clinton News Herald*, August 17, 2018. https://www.portclintonnewsherald.com/story/news/local/2018/08/17/elmore-ghost-tours-scaring-up-some-good-times/1017820002/.

Smith, Kristina. "Group Investigates Elmore Rider and Other Haunting Tales." *Port Clinton News Herald*, September 18, 2014. https://www.portclintonnewsherald.com/story/news/local/2014/09/17/group-investigates-elmore-rider-haunting-tales/15803129/.

St. James, Emily. "How The X-Files Invented Modern Television." Vox. October 23, 2018. https://www.vox.com/culture/2018/10/23/17989508/x-files-25th-anniversary-monsters-of-the-week-excerpt-todd-vanderwerff.

Traynor, Jessica. "How Tales of the Headless Horseman Came from Celtic Mythology." *Irish Times*, October 23, 2019. https://www.irishtimes.com/life-and-style/abroad/how-tales-of-the-headless-horseman-came-from-celtic-mythology-1.4060086.

Audio and Visual Resources

Ackroyd, Dan, Randy Lofficer and Harold Ramis. "The Headless Horseman." *The Real Ghostbusters*. Season 2, episode 37. Aired November 3, 1987. YouTube video. https://www.youtube.com/watch?v=m0pdpLTmwgE.

Gill, Daniel. "Elmore Rider Interview Part 1." YouTube video, 5:22. Posted February 14, 2021. https://www.youtube.com/watch?v=scqT4a9TNIU.

———. "Elmore Rider Interview Part 2." YouTube video, 8:18. Posted February 14, 2021. https://www.youtube.com/watch?v=1YXN-FL9SU8.

———. "Elmore Rider Interview Part 3." YouTube video, 7:02. Posted February 15, 2021. https://www.youtube.com/watch?v=pCx1GLx8ZmA.

Websites and Online Resources

IMDB. "*Kolchak: The Night Stalker*—'Chopper.'" https://www.imdb.com/title/tt0621534/.

Miami University Alumni Association. "Ghost Biker." https://www.miamialum.org/s/916/16/interior.aspx?pgid=415&gid=1&cid=26687.

Village of Elmore. "Village of Elmore." https://village.elmore.oh.us/.

8. Gore Orphanage

Books and Publications

Haines, Max. *Light and Hope: The Story of the Rev. John A. Sprunger and Katharina Sprunger*. N.p.: Self-published, 2021.
Tarrant, Rich. *Yesteryear in Vermilion Ohio*. Book 2. Victoria, BC: Trafford Press, 2005.
Willis, James A., Andrew Henderson and Loren Coleman. *Weird Ohio: Your Travel Guide to Ohio's Local Legends and Best Kept Secrets*. New York: Sterling Publishing Company Inc., 2005.

Newspapers

Toledo Blade *Vermilion News*

Interviews

Haines, Max (author of *Light and Hope: The Story of the Rev. John A. Sprunger and Katharina Sprunger*). Discussion with the author. June 18, 2022.
Tarrant, Rich (curator of the Vermilion History Museum). Discussion with the author. June 11, 2022.

Websites and Online Resources

Ritter Public Library. https://ritterpubliclibrary.org/.

9. The Legend of Holcomb Woods

Books and Publications

Coley, Joseph. *A Night on Holcomb Road*. Seattle, WA: Amazon, 2013. Kindle edition.

Articles

BG Falcon Media. "Haunted BG." February 25, 2021. https://www.bgfalconmedia.com/falcon_media_brands/bg_news/haunted-bg/article_b9facb17-eaa3-5cbd-bba5-2e824d6ed977.html.
Fringe Paranormal. "Holcomb Woods." June 28, 2018. https://fringeparanormal.wordpress.com/2018/06/28/holcomb-woods/.
LaPointe, Roger. "Holcomb Road Inspires Horror Film." *Sentinel-Tribune*, October 11, 2018. https://www.sent-trib.com/news/holcomb-road-inspires-horror-film/article_2223083c-cd50-11e8-af37-f36c41d63b30.html.

McGinnis, Jeff. "Legend Brought to Life—Wood County's Holcomb Road Folklore." *Toledo City Paper*, October 10, 2018. https://toledocitypaper.com/film/legend-brought-to-life-wood-countys-holcomb-road-folklore/.

Ohio Exploration Society. "Wood County Hauntings & Legends." https://www.ohioexploration.com/paranormal/hauntings/woodcounty/.

Stark, Kerrigan. "Ghost Stories: Creepy Legends of Wood County." BG Falcon Media. November 4, 2021.

Audio and Visual Sources

Capture 1 Studios. "Legend of Holcomb Road (Trailer)." YouTube video, 0:59. Posted August 17, 2018. https://www.youtube.com/watch?v=cxvkkwe0UJI.

10. MARITIME LEGENDS OF OHIO

Books and Publications

Heinsen, Victoria King. *Ghosts and Legends of Lake Erie's North Coast*. Charleston, SC: The History Press, 2010.

Manuscript Resources

Great Lakes Maritime Collection. Alpena County George N. Fletcher Public Library.
Historical Collections of the Great Lakes. Bowling Green State University.
Russell Brothers Ltd. Archives.

Newspapers and Periodicals

Chillicothe Gazette   *Steelcraft News*
Cleveland Herald   *Toledo Blade*
General Aviation News   *Toronto Star*
Port Clinton News Herald

Interviews

Heinsen, Victoria King (author of *Ghosts and Legends of Lake Erie's North Coast*). Discussion with the author. July 11, 2022.

Levya-Smith, Kelsey (Lorain County Port Authority office manager). Discussion with the author. July 22, 2022.

Websites and Online Resources

Lorain County Auditor's Office. https://www.loraincounty.com/auditor/.

Ohio Sea Grant. https://ohioseagrant.osu.edu/.

Ohio Secretary of State. https://www.sos.state.oh.us/.

Shipwrecks and Maritime Tales of Lake Erie Coastal Trail. http://www.ohioshipwrecks.org/.

USS *Sachem* 1902 Project. https://uss-sachem.org/.

11. The Portage County UFO Chase

Books and Publications

Hynek, J. Allen. *The Hynek UFO Report.* New York: Dell Publishing Company, 1977.

———. *The UFO Experience: A Scientific Inquiry.* Washington, D.C.: H. Regnery Company, 1972. Reprint, Boston: Da Capo Press, 1998.

Jacobsen, Annie. *Area 51: An Uncensored History of America's Top Secret Military Base.* Boston: Little, Brown and Company, 2011.

Pilkington, Mark. *Mirage Men: An Adventure into Paranoia, Espionage, Psychological Warfare, and UFOs.* New York: Skyhorse Publishing, 2010.

Quintanilla, Hector. *UFOs: An Air Force Dilemma.* 1975. Reprint, Las Vegas, NV: National Institute of Discovery Science, 2016.

Renner, James. *It Came from Ohio…: True Tales of the Weird, Wild, and Unexplained.* Cleveland, OH: Gray & Company, Publishers, 2012.

Ruppelt, Edward J. *The Report on Unidentified Flying Objects.* New York: Doubleday & Company, 1956.

Weitzel, William B. *The P-13 UFO: Summary Report on April 17, 1966 UFO Chase from Portage County, Ohio, into Conway, Pennsylvania.* Pittsburgh, PA: Pittsburgh Investigative Subcommittee, National Investigations Committee on Aerial Phenomena, June 28, 1966.

Manuscript Resources

Cleveland Plain Dealer. "Spaur." May 10, 1984. Center for Local & Global History. Cleveland Public Library.

Gerald R. Ford Presidential Library. "Ford Press Releases—UFO, 1966." Ford Congressional Papers: Press Secretary and Speech File. https://www.fordlibrarymuseum.gov/library/document/0054/4525586.pdf.

UFO History Files. "Goodyear UFO Society Note." http://ufohistoryfiles.com/wp-content/uploads/2014/08/146C.pdf.

United States Air Force. "Project 10073 Record." Project Blue Book. Retrieved from the Black Vault. https://documents2.theblackvault.com/documents/projectbluebook/ProjectBlueBook-April171966-Ravenna-Mantua-Ohio.pdf.

Newspapers and Periodicals

Akron Beacon Journal	*New York Dispatch*
Associated Press	*Philadelphia Inquirer*
Cincinnati Enquirer	*Pittsburgh Press*
Cincinnati Post	*Port Clinton News Herald*
Dayton Daily News	*San Angelo Standard-Times*
Dover Daily Reporter	*Sandusky Register*
Hamilton Journal News	*Spokane Spokesman Review*
Hubbard News Recorder	United Press International
Kent Stater	*Victoria* (British Columbia) *Daily Times*
Mansfield News Journal	*Zanesville Times Recorder*
Marion Star	

Articles

Dix, David. "Along the Way." Record Courier, July 13, 2014. https://www.record-courier.com/story/opinion/2014/07/13/along-way-david-dix/19947339007/.

Patterson, Jeff. "Something Happened to Dale." Medium. November 29, 2021. https://medium.com/on-the-trail-of-the-saucers/something-happened-to-dale-68c2ac39d5a8.

Renner, James. "Strangers in the Night." Cleveland Scene, March 31, 2004. https://www.clevescene.com/news/strangers-in-the-night-1485939.

Rense. "Cops Chase UFO—'Seven Steps to Hell' Enigma Solved." https://rense.com/general70/copsd.htm.

Wolford, Ben. "Seeing a UFO Ruined Dale Spaur's Life." Medium. January 9, 2018. https://medium.com/the-portager/seeing-a-ufo-ruined-dale-spaurs-life-f86bab152368.

Audio and Visual Resources

SpaceTimeForum. "Interview with Deputy Sheriff Dale Spaur 1966." YouTube video, 18:40. Posted March 28, 2013. https://www.youtube.com/watch?v=aHJcCCUdotw.

Spielberg, Steven. *Close Encounters of the Third Kind.* Culver City, CA: Columbia Pictures, 1977. DVD.

UFO History. "Portage County, Ohio, April 17, 1966. NICAP_s William Weitzel asked Dale Spaur, etc." YouTube video, 14:35. Posted October 7, 2018. https://www.youtube.com/watch?v=A4JEGMpwmKI.

Websites and Online Resources

Ancestry. "Dale F. Spaur—Death Record." Ohio Department of Health. Ohio, U.S., Death Records, 1908–1932, 1938–2018 (database online). https://www.

ancestryinstitution.com/discoveryui-content/view/1352981:5763?tid=&p
 id=&queryId=86ad502f05986088abc11e992ad92091&_phsrc=avg11&_
 phstart=successSource.

Find a Grave. "Dale Floyd Spaur." https://www.findagrave.com/
 memorial/126594969/dale-floyd-spaur.

Google Maps. "Randolph, Ohio, to Conway, Pennsylvania." www.google.com/maps.

Heavens Above. "Echo 1 Orbit." https://www.heavens-above.com/orbit.
 aspx?satid=00049.

———. "Echo 2 Orbit." https://www.heavens-above.com/orbit.aspx?satid=00740.

National Aeronautics and Space Administration. "Project Echo." https://www.
 nasa.gov/centers/langley/about/project-echo.html.

12. THE WOW! SIGNAL

Newspapers

Columbus Dispatch   *Newsletter*
North American Astrophysical Observatory

Interviews

Brown, Greg (Armstrong Air and Space Museum historian and collections
 coordinator). Discussion with the author. March 18, 2022.

Stevens, Don (director of Perkins Observatory). Discussions with the author. April
 29, 2022, and June 7, 2022.

Websites and Online Resources

North American Astrophysical Observatory Big Ear Memorial Website. http://
 www.bigear.org/.

13. THE COYNE UFO INCIDENT

Books and Publications

Zeidman, Jennie. *A Helicopter-UFO Encounter Over Ohio.* Evanston, IL: Center for
 UFO Studies, 1979.

Newspapers and Periodicals

Indianapolis Star   *FATE Magazine*
International UFO Reporter

Interviews

Rodeghier, Mark (president and scientific director of the Center for UFO Studies). Discussion with the author. March 16, 2022.

EPILOGUE

Books and Publications

Godfrey, Linda S. *I Know What I Saw: Modern-Day Encounters with Monsters of New Urban Legend and Ancient Lore.* New York: Penguin Publishing Group, 2020.

Articles

Kluger, Jeffrey. "Congress Is Finally Taking UFOs Seriously, 50 Years After Its Last Hearing on the Mysterious Subject." *TIME*, May 17, 2022.

ABOUT THE AUTHORS

As a child, M. Kristina Smith read every book on the Loch Ness Monster she could find at the Defiance Public Library. Since then, she has been interested in cryptids, the paranormal and unexplained phenomena.

As a former investigative reporter and editor, she spent years asking questions, digging through public records and researching materials to find the facts behind stories. Today, she shares the history and stories of the collections, people and events at the Rutherford B. Hayes Presidential Library and Museums, where she has been a marketing/communications manager since 2015. She also works as a freelance writer and reporter, featuring stories about people, wildlife and places around Ohio.

This is her second book. Her first, *Lost Sandusky*, was published by The History Press in 2015.

Kevin has been writing since he was eight years old, pecking away on his mom's typewriter. He enjoys reading and writing fiction, and maybe one day, he will write the great American novel— but not today. Kevin decided to pivot his life toward studying history professionally about ten years ago and hasn't looked back since. He now gets to research, preserve and share history as the curator of artifacts at the Rutherford B. Hayes Presidential Library and Museums in Fremont, Ohio. He also hosts *Can't Make*

This Up: A History Podcast, where he gets the privilege of interviewing authors and historians. Kevin lives in Toledo with his family.

Visit us at
www.historypress.com